Family Fare

Family Fare

Christelle Erasmus & Eric Barnard

Human & Rousseau
Cape Town   Pretoria

First edition, first impression 1993
Second impression 2001
Second edition, first impression 2007 by Human & Rousseau
An imprint of NB Publishers
40 Heerengracht, Cape Town 8000

Publisher: Tania de Kock
Editor: Madeleine Barnard
Design: Nathalie Scott
Photography: Neville Lockhart
Styling: Kanya Hunt
Recipe preparation: Alana Erasmus

Reproduction by Unifoto Pty (Ltd), Cape Town
Printed and bound by Tien Wah (Pte) Ltd, Singapore

ISBN-10   0-7981-4798-9
ISBN-13   978-0-7981-4798-9

Contents

FOREWORD

Providing a hearty, nourishing meal for your family every evening is not the easiest thing to do. I think that most moms will agree with me on this one! Time and money are of vital importance.

And this is the reason why I started this concept years ago. I started experimenting with recipes and soon discovered that this necessitated planning each month's meals in advance to ensure that I would have all the ingredients at hand – I simply could not afford those expensive mid-month shopping trips to the corner café. This method produced astonishing results: we enjoyed better meals than ever before, Coen, my husband, was lavish with his praise and, to top it all, the monthly food bill was much lower. Cooking, which had always been a burden, now become a pleasure.

After the birth of my first daughter, I started working again, and with less time on my hands, I reverted back to my old ways – no menus, no advance planning. Each morning, on my way to work, I would start agonising about what to cook for supper. Having eventually decided on a supper menu, I would then get home to find that half the required ingredients were absent from the grocery cupboard. All the frustrations of cooking were back, and this time with a vengeance. I realised that a well-planned menu, with a variety of dishes and a comprehensive shopping list for each month, was the only solution. Since then, this system has become part of our lives. I'll never deviate from it again.

Our friends, Eric and Agnes, were very keen to implement this concept in their household as well, especially with food prices on the increase all the time. Their domestic helper, who does the cooking during the week, welcomed the idea with enthusiasm. Now Eric and Agnes compile the menu at the beginning of each month, do the shopping and leave the rest to the cook! And the best of all, Eric manages to save more on food than I do.

Eric and I wrote this book to help other families save time and money in today's difficult economic climate. I believe that anyone who takes these ideas to heart, will come to view cooking in a different light: no more drudgery, but sheer pleasure!

It is now 13 years since the book was first published, and what a pleasure to discover that *Family Fare* is still fulfilling a truly respected role in the lives of my children and their friends. *Family Fare* is a concept that keeps on working!

Christelle Erasmus

Christelle Erasmus
Cape Town, August 2006

INTRODUCTION

Preparing a nourishing supper for her family every evening is quite a problem for the modern woman, with her full daily programme. Because she doesn't have the time to try out new recipes, her family gets the same tried and tested dishes year in and year out. No wonder that cooking has become a drudgery for many of us!

Careful planning of meals can make the daily task much easier and more interesting. This book should help everyone to break out of a boring and predictable cooking pattern, and save time and money as well. The dishes are ordinary homely fare without any frills, and for this reason should find favour with the whole family.

Menus

Family Fare contains twelve monthly menus which feature the main meal for each day. Should a certain day's menu not be suitable due to lack of time, it can be exchanged for another day in the same month.

At the start of each day's menu, there's a box in which to write the date. So, for example, if the first day of the month falls on a Thursday, write the figure "1" in the appropriate box, "2" in Friday's box, and so on until the last day of the month, which in this case will be the Wednesday of the first week.

The monthly menus can also be exchanged, but remember that some of the fruit and vegetables are seasonal and can thus be considerably more expensive in another month of the year.

We have not followed a set pattern of certain kinds of meat on specified days. Sometimes a specific type of meat is repeated during one week, especially in the case of chicken which is so versatile that it is never boring.

The menus are put together in such a way that lighter meals with salads appear about three times a week. "Leftovers" appear at least once a month; it need not be the previous day's food. Sometimes a day is skipped on the menu, for example when the family is away from home for some or other reason, or one or more family members are absent or ill and there are thus leftover portions which can be stored for later use. That day's food can be prepared on the "leftover" days.

The desserts for the month are given at the end of each monthly menu. You can decide for yourself on which days desserts will be served. The ingredients for the desserts are also included on the shopping lists.

YOUR OWN MENUS FOR SPECIAL OCCASIONS: We have allowed two pages at the end of the menu section of the book on which you can write your own favourite menus for special guests, family occasions and so on.

Purchases

At the end of each month's menus, there is a shopping list for the month concerned. **This includes all products needed for the main meals for the month. Note that fresh produce that should be bought daily or weekly does not appear on this list but on the menu.**

This shopping list makes it possible for you to work more economically. You will save time and money by not having to run to the corner café every five minutes to buy something you've forgotten. And because you're buying to a plan, the pantry will also not become overfull. Another plus is that any family member can do the monthly shopping using the list, which gives you breathing space.

FRESH PRODUCTS: A number of fresh products have to be bought daily or weekly. To make planning easier, the fresh products for each day are given in a separate column alongside the menu concerned. Decide for yourself how often to buy fresh products, and consult the list on a regular basis.

HERBS AND SPICES: All the herbs and spices for the month are given on the shopping list. As these products keep for months, the list is simply a master list to make sure that you have these specific herbs or spices in your store cupboard.

MEAT: Meat purchases are made only for the month concerned. The sizes of the packs vary according to the size of the family and are so indicated. If "braai" appears on the menu and sausage is not added, for example, we use 8-12 portions of meat instead of the usual 6-8 portions.

GENERAL: The greater majority of products are listed under this heading. Remember that not all cans come in standard sizes; if you cannot find the size listed, buy a can that's the closest in size.

We have left space for notes on each month's shopping list. Special occasions like birthdays, weddings, anniversaries, and so on can be noted here to remind you to buy gifts or cards.

GENERAL MONTHLY MASTER LIST: The list at the front of the book is simply a master list for additional purchases. It's a good idea to check, every now and then, on stocks of vinegar, Worcester sauce, tomato sauce, chutney and so on in your cupboard before buying for the next month.

On this list there are also a number of products – e.g. sugar and margarine, for – which are already on the monthly shopping list.

Remember that the monthly shopping list refers only to products needed for the menus. There is thus a good deal of space for your own notes about breakfast, lunch, snacks, general household purchases and so on.

Breakfast and lunch

Each family's needs and circumstances are different, and that's why breakfast and lunch are not included in our monthly menus. Some families enjoy a hearty breakfast (fruit juice, porridge, bacon and eggs) and sandwiches later in the day. Others cannot face anything more than rusks with coffee or tea early in the morning, but then take sandwiches, fruit and cheese with them for teatime and lunch. If mum is at home when the kids come home from school, she will make something light in the afternoon. Maybe parents often go on business lunches and prefer something light for breakfast and supper on those days.

It doesn't take much effort to plan and budget for breakfast and lunch, and for snacks.

YOUR OWN MENUS FOR BREAKFAST AND LUNCH: Make a note of everything your family eats for breakfast and lunch (and in between) for a week. Calculate how much will be needed for a month, and add it to your monthly shopping list. You should be reasonably accurate at the first attempt, although it will probably take you two or three months to perfect .

- Buy smaller quantities and a greater variety, if possible.
- Note at which main meals there are generally leftovers and allow for this in your planning.

- Use leftovers creatively: as a filling for sandwiches, potatoes or omelettes, or in a salad.
- Remember that figure-conscious or growing teenagers have changing needs.
- Find out from your family what they like in particular and try to vary meals.

Recipes

All the recipes are for a family of four to six people. All the dishes on the menus and elsewhere for which a recipe is given are marked with an asterisk (*). If a recipe freezes well and is doubled for use later in the month it is marked with "##" after the name.

Quantities are sometimes given in the same way as on the shopping list: 6-8 slices bread. The quantity will be determined by the size of the family.

MICROWAVE METHOD: All the recipes in this book are written for preparation on the stove, with the microwave method given as an alternative here and there.

Microwave ovens are not standardised and can differ from one another. Where the alternative microwave method is given, the recipe was tested in a 600 watt microwave oven.

Lunchbox tips

The lunchbox will need close attention if both mum and dad go out to work and the children go to school.

- *Include fresh fruit with sandwiches — it is always popular.*
- *Dried fruit is the obvious alternative during the months when fresh fruit is not as freely available; or what about a fruit bar for those with a sweet tooth?*
- *Strips of fresh vegetables are delicious in a packed lunch. Many children who refuse to eat cooked vegetables can be persuaded to eat vegetables in this form.*
- *Making sandwiches every day is no joke. Although it's fun to experiment with unusual fillings from time to time, experience shows us that most children prefer the familiar ones.*
- *In the section "Bread and its companions" there are a few favourite sandwich fillings; some with surprising combinations of ingredients.*

Tips that work:

- Always take a coolbag with you when you go shopping to keep frozen foods and other perishables from spoiling on the way home.
- Pack meat in meal-size portions before freezing.
- Freeze the second batches of doubled recipes (##) in the dish in which they will be served. Line the dish with tinfoil or plastic wrap and spoon in the food. Allow to chill, then seal and freeze.
- Use cottage cheese and margarine tubs to freeze smaller quantities of leftover food or soup.
- Disposable "wipes" are a marvellous substitute for coffee filter papers. Soak them in boiling water first — they can be used over and over again.
- Add a pinch of bicarbonate of soda to milk to keep it fresh.
- Keep lemon peels for bath time: throw the peels in the bath and turn on the hot-water tap. The water will have a refreshing smell and your skin will feel soft and smooth.
- A thin layer of sugar in the bottom of the cake tin will help to keep biscuits fresh and crisp.
- Biscuits that have become soft can be baked in the oven for a few minutes. Allow them to cool and repack them in the cake tin.
- Eggs keep longer if stored in the refrigerator.
- Make sure that you aren't paying more for a product simply because it's packed in an attractive container.
- Individually packed biscuits, tea bags and so on are convenient but considerably more expensive.
- Bread, rolls and cakes all freeze well.
- Grate a supply of Cheddar cheese and freeze it in an airtight container. Use as required.
- Use a sauce to combine leftovers and transform them into a tasty meal.
- When cleaning the house, carry a basket around with you and place in it all the bits and pieces that are lying around; it will save you much toing and froing.
- Use an old woollen sock for buffing.
- Don't throw away small pieces of soap. Place them in an old stocking and tie it to an outside tap for washing hands.
- To save electricity, turn down the thermostat on the hot-water cylinder during the summer months.
- Keep all glass bottles with lids and use them for jam and canned fruit.
- To keep lettuce fresh, store it in a plastic shopping bag in the refrigerator.
- Store fresh fruit and vegetables in the refrigerator during the summer months.
- To save time and money, buy vegetables like green beans and carrots in bulk when they are cheaper and freeze them for the times when they are expensive and scarce.
- Don't boil more water in the kettle than you need; a full kettle uses more electricity.
- Use your microwave oven as often as possible to save electricity.
- Test the shorter cycles on your washing machine to save water and electricity; it isn't always necessary to use the longer cycles.
- In rooms that are not often used, use low wattage globes instead of high.
- Place cleaned fresh garlic in a jar of oil and store in the refrigerator. The garlic will keep fresh for a long time and the oil can be used in a salad dressing.

General monthly master list

FRUIT AND VEGETABLES

- [ ] Fruit
- [ ] Potatoes
- [ ] Onions
- [ ] Tomatoes
- [ ] Cucumber
- [ ] Lettuce
- [ ] Pumpkin
- [ ] Squash
- [ ] Cabbage
- [ ] Green beans
- [ ] Carrots

_____
_____
_____
_____
_____
_____
_____
_____

FRESH DAIRY PRODUCTS

- [ ] Milk
- [ ] Cheddar cheese
- [ ] Feta cheese
- [ ] Mozzarella cheese
- [ ] Cream cheese
- [ ] Cottage cheese
- [ ] Cream
- [ ] Yoghurt
- [ ] Margarine
- [ ] Eggs

_____
_____
_____
_____
_____
_____
_____

COLD AND FROZEN PRODUCTS

- [ ] Bacon
- [ ] Cold meats
- [ ] Processed sausage
- [ ] Frozen vegetables
- [ ] Chicken
- [ ] Fish
- [ ] Meat patties
- [ ] Fruit juice
- [ ] Ice cream
- [ ] Sausage
- [ ] Meat

_____
_____
_____
_____
_____
_____

DRY PRODUCTS

- [ ] Sugar
- [ ] Rice
- [ ] Soup powder
- [ ] Cake flour
- [ ] Cornflour
- [ ] Baking powder
- [ ] Self-raising flour
- [ ] Icing sugar
- [ ] Custard powder
- [ ] Jelly powder
- [ ] Instant pudding
- [ ] Spaghetti
- [ ] Macaroni
- [ ] Noodles
- [ ] Cereals
- [ ] Oats
- [ ] Rusks
- [ ] Biscuits

_____
_____
_____
_____
_____

SAUCES AND FLAVOURINGS

- [ ] Tomato sauce
- [ ] Chutney
- [ ] Mayonnaise
- [ ] Soy sauce
- [ ] Worcester sauce
- [ ] Vinegar
- [ ] Oil
- [ ] Herbs
- [ ] Spices
- [ ] Meat stock
- [ ] Jam
- [ ] Spreads
- [ ] Syrup

CANNED FOOD

- [ ] Tuna
- [ ] Sardines
- [ ] Curried fish
- [ ] Corned beef
- [ ] Tomato and onion mix
- [ ] Tomato purée
- [ ] Tomato paste
- [ ] Asparagus
- [ ] Mushrooms
- [ ] Beans in tomato sauce
- [ ] Creamstyle sweetcorn
- [ ] Peas
- [ ] Fruit
- [ ] Evaporated milk
- [ ] Condensed milk

DRINKS

- [ ] Coffee
- [ ] Tea
- [ ] Cool drink
- [ ] Lemon juice
- [ ] Fruit juice
- [ ] Milo

TOILETRIES

- [ ] Toothpaste
- [ ] Toilet soap
- [ ] Soap
- [ ] Shampoo
- [ ] Hair spray
- [ ] Shaving cream
- [ ] Blades
- [ ] Deodorant
- [ ] Sanitary towels
- [ ] Hand and body lotion
- [ ] First aid products
- [ ] Toilet paper

CLEANING MATERIALS

- [ ] Washing powder
- [ ] Fabric softener
- [ ] Bleach
- [ ] Dishwashing liquid
- [ ] All-purpose cleaner
- [ ] Furniture polish
- [ ] Shoe polish
- [ ] Oven cleaner
- [ ] Air freshener
- [ ] Insecticide

GENERAL

- [ ] Pet food
- [ ] Scourers
- [ ] Dish towels
- [ ] Kitchen swabs
- [ ] Batteries
- [ ] Paper towels
- [ ] Serviettes
- [ ] Aluminium foil
- [ ] Plastic bags
- [ ] Waxed paper
- [ ] Swimming pool products
- [ ] Firelighters

Notes

January

MENU	FRESH PRODUCE
MON — Chicken in wine*, yellow rice with raisins, peas, cauliflower with white sauce*, beetroot salad	*Cauliflower, milk, beetroot (if preferred fresh)*
TUES — Pizza for Africa* (pineapple and ham)	*200 g mozzarella cheese, 200 g Cheddar cheese*
WED — Sausage, mashed potatoes, beans in tomato sauce, peas	*4-6 large potatoes, milk*
THURS — Macaroni cheese*, mixed salad	*150 g Cheddar cheese, 2 tomatoes, 500 ml milk, vegetables for salad*
FRI — Tuna noodle salad*, sweet melon, watermelon	*1 tomato, 1 green pepper, 1 apple, lettuce, sweet melon, watermelon, 1 onion*
SAT — Lamb chops, tomato and onion toasts, mealies, mixed salad	*2 tomatoes, 1 onion, 4-6 mealies, vegetables for salad, 8-12 slices bread*
SUN — Braaied chicken (King Arthur's chicken marinade*), Estelle's rice salad*, carrot salad, sliced cucumber	*1 green pepper, 2 onions, 1 tomato, carrots, 2 oranges (if desired in carrot salad), cucumber*
MON — Leftovers (clean out refrigerator) and cheese and tomato toasts	*2 tomatoes, 8-12 slices bread, 100 g Cheddar cheese*
TUES — Fish lasagne*, mixed salad	*1 onion, 100 g Cheddar cheese, vegetables for salad*
WED — Frikkadels*, baked potatoes, orange sweet potatoes*, green beans	*2 slices white bread, 6-8 potatoes, 2 carrots, green beans, 2 onions, milk, 4-5 sweet potatoes, 1 orange*
THURS — Bake-in-a-bag chicken*, rice, peas, carrot salad, sweet melon	*Carrots, 2 oranges (if desired in carrot salad), sweet melon*
FRI — Bacon and banana toasts	*10-16 slices bread, 5 ripe bananas*
SAT — Braaied sausage, rolls, mealies	*4-6 rolls, 4-6 mealies*
SUN — Braaied lamb chops, quick bean salad*, sweet melon, jacket potatoes	*6-8 potatoes, 1 onion, sweet melon*
MON — Spaghetti bolognaise*, mixed salad	*1 onion, 200 g Cheddar cheese, vegetables for salad*
TUES — Chicken Tetrazzini*, mixed salad, sweet melon	*2 onions, 250 g button mushrooms, 375 ml milk, 150 g Cheddar cheese, vegetables for salad, sweet melon*
WED — Smoorsnoek dish*, mixed salad	*1 onion, 1 lemon (optional), vegetables for salad*

Day	Meal	Ingredients
THURS	Cottage pie*, green beans, sweet pumpkin*	5 potatoes, 2 onions, 200 ml milk, green beans, 750 g "boer" pumpkin or butternut
FRI	Hamburgers, chips	6 – 8 large potatoes, 1 tomato, onion, lettuce, 4-6 rolls
SAT	Braaied chicken (King Arthur's chicken marinade*), sliced pineapple, rolls, watermelon (Braai 3 extra pieces of chicken for chicken and asparagus tart*, later in the month)	1 onion, 1 pineapple, 4-6 rolls, watermelon
SUN	Melt-in-the-mouth steak*, rice, baby marrow stir-fry*, creamy squash*, beetroot salad	Beetroot (if preferred fresh), 2-3 squash, cream (optional), 1 onion, 1 tomato, 400 g baby marrows
MON	Mince surprise*, carrot salad, sweet melon	1 onion, carrots, 2 oranges (if desired in carrot salad), sweet melon
TUES	Macaroni cheese*, mixed salad	150 g Cheddar cheese, 2 tomatoes, 500 ml milk, vegetables for salad
WED	Hake with yoghurt sauce*, mashed potatoes, peas, beans in tomato sauce	50 g Cheddar cheese, 175 ml milk, 125 ml plain yoghurt, 5-7 potatoes
THURS	Frikkadels*, yellow rice with raisins, green beans, mealies	Green beans, 4-6 mealies
FRI	Chicken and asparagus tart*, mixed salad, carrot salad	250 ml milk, 50 g Cheddar cheese, vegetables for salad, carrots, 2 oranges (if desired in carrot salad)
SAT	Braaied sausage, mealies, potatoes in onion sauce*, mixed salad	4-6 mealies, 6 large potatoes, vegetables for salad
SUN	Apricot chicken*, spicy rice*, peas, cauliflower with white sauce*, beetroot salad	Cauliflower, milk, beetroot (if preferred fresh)
MON	Leftovers (clean out refrigerator)	
TUES	Tuna noodle salad*, whole-wheat bread	1 tomato, 1 onion, 1 green pepper, 1 apple, lettuce, whole-wheat bread
WED	Chicken Tetrazzini*, mixed salad	Vegetables for salad

Desserts

Trifle*	1 trifle sponge, 1,25 litres milk, 250 ml cream
Ice-cream surprise*	250 ml cream, 4 bananas, meringues
Jelly and custard	500 ml milk
Chocolate peaches*	
Ice cream with chocolate sauce*	
Fruit salad and ice cream	Fruit for fruit salad

Shopping list

SPICES AND HERBS

- [ ] Salt
- [ ] Black pepper
- [ ] Cayenne pepper
- [ ] Turmeric
- [ ] Ground cinnamon
- [ ] Curry powder
- [ ] Oregano
- [ ] Garlic flakes
- [ ] Paprika
- [ ] Mixed spice
- [ ] Flavour enhancer
- [ ] Thyme
- [ ] Parsley
- [ ] Nutmeg
- [ ] Spice for rice

_____
_____
_____
_____
_____
_____

MEAT AND FISH

- [ ] 2 packets (6-8 pieces each) chicken portions
- [ ] 2 packets (8-12 pieces each) chicken portions
- [ ] 1 packet (3 pieces) chicken portions
- [ ] 2 whole chickens
- [ ] 250 g ham (any kind)
- [ ] 2 x 250 g diced bacon
- [ ] 3 x sausage
- [ ] 5 x 500 g mince
- [ ] 1 packet hamburger patties
- [ ] 1 kg tenderised steak
- [ ] 2 packets (8-12 pieces each) lamb chops
- [ ] 1 packet (800 g) hake fillets

_____
_____
_____
_____
_____
_____

GENERAL

- [ ] 1 kg Cheddar cheese (omit if cheese is bought weekly – see fresh produce on menu)
- [ ] 200 g mozzarella cheese (omit if cheese is bought weekly – see fresh produce on menu)
- [ ] 1,5 kg margarine
- [ ] 250 g butter
- [ ] 2 dozen eggs
- [ ] 1 bottle Worcester sauce
- [ ] 1 bottle tomato sauce
- [ ] 2 bottles cooking oil
- [ ] 2 bottles chutney
- [ ] 750 ml mayonnaise
- [ ] 2 packets chicken marinade
- [ ] 2 packets brown onion soup powder
- [ ] 4 packets cream of mushroom soup powder
- [ ] 1 can (410 g) tomato soup
- [ ] 1 can (410 g) minestrone
- [ ] 3 kg rice
- [ ] 400 g macaroni
- [ ] 2 packets (500 g each) shell noodles
- [ ] 375 g spinach noodles
- [ ] 1 packet spaghetti
- [ ] 1 kg flour
- [ ] 500 g self-raising flour
- [ ] 1 container custard powder
- [ ] 1 can cocoa
- [ ] cream of tartar
- [ ] 1 bottle vanilla essence
- [ ] 2,5 kg sugar
- [ ] 250 g seedless raisins
- [ ] 125 ml chopped walnuts (optional for trifle)
- [ ] 1 can (400 g) smoorsnoek
- [ ] 6 cans (200 g each) tuna
- [ ] 2 small cans (225 g each) mixed vegetables
- [ ] 6 cans (410 g each) or 2,1 kg frozen peas
- [ ] 1 can (410 g) asparagus
- [ ] 2 cans (410 g each) tomato and onion mix
- [ ] 1 can (410 g) tomato purée
- [ ] 3 cans (420 g each) beans in tomato sauce
- [ ] 3 bottles beetroot salad (omit if fresh beetroot is bought)

- [ ] 1 can (440 g) pineapple pieces
- [ ] 1 can (410 g) sliced peaches
- [ ] 1 can (820 g) peach halves in syrup
- [ ] 1 can (410 g) fruit salad
- [ ] 1 small can apricot jam
- [ ] 1 can golden syrup
- [ ] 1 can (410 g) evaporated milk
- [ ] 1 can cream
- [ ] 1 carton (250 ml) apricot juice
- [ ] 1 packet jelly (any kind)
- [ ] 1 packet red jelly
- [ ] 1 packet green jelly
- [ ] 1 litre vanilla ice cream
- [ ] 1 litre ice cream (any flavour)
- [ ] 1 Peppermint Crisp
- [ ] 1 packet Choc Crust biscuits
- [ ] 100 g Chick a Bix biscuits
- [ ] 1 medium-sized cooking bag
- [ ] 150 ml sweet wine
- [ ] 250 ml white wine

Notes and birthdays

	MENU	FRESH PRODUCE
MON	Tuna salad*, whole-wheat crispbread with cheese	*1 tomato, lettuce, 1 pineapple, cheese*
TUES	Cape pear chicken*, bacon beans*, carrots, potatoes	*500 g green beans, 4-6 carrots, 4-6 potatoes*
WED	Cottage pie*, squash, peas, mixed salad	*5 potatoes, 1 onion, milk, 2-3 squash, vegetables for salad*
THURS	Lamb neck casserole*, cauliflower with cheese, pumpkin, rice, carrot salad	*2 onions, cauliflower, 100 g Cheddar cheese, pumpkin, carrots, 2 oranges (if desired in carrot salad)*
FRI	Fish (cold), rice salad*, tomato salad*, whole-wheat bread	*4-5 tomatoes, 2 onions, 3 bananas, 1 green pepper, pineapple, whole-wheat bread*
SAT	Quick cheese snacks*, mixed salad	*8-10 slices rye bread, 100 g Cheddar cheese, 250 g smooth cottage cheese, vegetables for salad*
SUN	Braai (lamb chops, sausage), braai bread, banana and bean salad*	*3 bananas, 8-12 slices bread, cheese and tomato for braai bread*
MON	Fish cakes*, mashed potatoes, peas, carrots (Prepare Ina's salad delight* for Wednesday)	*1 onion, 4-6 potatoes, milk, 4-6 carrots*
TUES	Pasta à la Alrina*, mixed salad	*1 onion, 250 g button mushrooms, vegetables for salad*
WED	Steak, chips, Ina's salad delight*, sweet melon	*6-8 potatoes, pineapple, 1 onion, 1 sweet melon*
THURS	Sweet and tangy chicken*, potatoes, green beans, mealies, beetroot salad	*5-7 potatoes, green beans, mealies, beetroot (if preferred fresh)*
FRI	Mince curry*, toast	*1 onion, 2 carrots, 1 green apple, 2 large potatoes, 8-12 slices bread*
SAT	Sweet-and-sour pork*, rice, mixed salad	*1 green pepper, vegetables for salad*
SUN	Braai (lamb ribs, sausage), bread rolls, sliced pineapple, sweet melon	*Bread rolls, pineapple, sweet melon*
MON	Cottage pie*, green beans, glazed carrots, mixed salad (Prepare Mum's curried peach salad* for Tuesday)	*Milk, 5 potatoes, 1 onion, green beans, 4-6 carrots, vegetables for salad*
TUES	Fish (cold), jacket potatoes (cold), beetroot salad, Mum's curried peach salad*	*4-6 potatoes, 2 onions, beetroot (if preferred fresh)*
WED	Pan-fried pork chops, savoury rice*, spinach, stewed dried fruit, mixed salad	*Spinach, vegetables for salad*

Day	Meal	Ingredients
THURS	Apricot chicken*, potatoes, broccoli, carrots, tomato salad*	4-6 potatoes, broccoli, 4-6 carrots, 3-4 tomatoes, 2 onions
FRI	Agnes's noodles*, mixed salad	1 onion, 1 green pepper, 1 tomato, 100 g Cheddar cheese, vegetables for salad
SAT	Braai (steak), garlic bread*, potato bake*, mixed salad	1 French loaf, 6 potatoes, 250 ml fresh cream, vegetables for salad
SUN	Cold meats, bread rolls, carrot salad, sweet melon, rice salad*, sliced tomatoes	Bread rolls, carrots, 2 oranges (if desired for carrot salad), 3 bananas, 1 green pepper, pineapple, 3 tomatoes, 1 sweet melon
MON	Lasagne*, mixed salad	2 onions, 1 green pepper, 1 clove garlic, 80 g Cheddar cheese, 500 ml milk, vegetables for salad
TUES	Sausage, mashed potatoes, peas, marshmallow squash*, carrot salad	4-6 potatoes, milk, 3-4 squash, carrots, 2 oranges (if desired for carrot salad)
WED	Roast chicken, potatoes, sweet pumpkin*, green beans	4-6 potatoes, green beans, 750 g "boer" pumpkin or butternut, 1 onion
THURS	Pizza for Africa* (bacon and mushrooms)	250 g button mushrooms, 200 g Cheddar cheese, 200 g mozzarella cheese
FRI	Fish fingers, eggs, banana and bean salad*, bread rolls (Prepare Ina's salad delight* for Sunday)	3 bananas, bread rolls
SAT	Tipsy lamb potjie*, rice, mealies	2 onions, 4-6 potatoes, 4-5 carrots, 250 g button mushrooms, 250 g baby marrows, mealies
SUN	Braai (lamb chops, sausage), cheese and tomato braai bread, Ina's salad delight*	8-12 slices bread, 2 tomatoes for braai bread, cheese, 1 onion, pineapple
MON	Leftovers (clean out refrigerator)	

Desserts

Ice cream with chocolate sauce*	
Fruit salad	Fresh fruit
Madelein's cold pudding*	
Karen's pineapple tart*	
Jelly and custard	500 ml milk
Banana with custard	Bananas, 500 ml milk

Shopping list

SPICES AND HERBS

- [ ] Flavour enhancer
- [ ] Black pepper
- [ ] Paprika
- [ ] Nutmeg
- [ ] Parsley
- [ ] Oregano
- [ ] Mild curry powder
- [ ] Turmeric
- [ ] Mixed herbs
- [ ] Basil
- [ ] Garlic powder
- [ ] Thyme
- [ ] Ground coriander

_____
_____
_____
_____
_____
_____

MEAT AND FISH

- [ ] 4 packets (6-8 pieces each) chicken portions
- [ ] 1 x 750 g mince
- [ ] 3 x 500 g mince
- [ ] 1,25 kg lamb neck chops
- [ ] 2 x 800 g hake
- [ ] 2 packets (6-8 pieces each) lamb chops
- [ ] 4 x 500 g sausage
- [ ] 2 packets (4-6 pieces each) steak
- [ ] 750 g pork fillet, cubed
- [ ] 1 kg lamb rib
- [ ] 6-8 pork chops
- [ ] 1,25 kg lamb knuckles
- [ ] 3 x 250 g rindless bacon
- [ ] 500 g mixed cold meats

_____
_____
_____
_____
_____

GENERAL

- [ ] 500 g Cheddar cheese (omit if bought weekly – see fresh produce on menu)
- [ ] 200 g mozzarella cheese (omit if bought weekly – see fresh produce on menu)
- [ ] 250 g smooth cottage cheese (omit if bought weekly – see fresh produce on menu)
- [ ] 1 kg margarine
- [ ] 1 litre ice cream
- [ ] 500 g frozen fish fingers
- [ ] 3 dozen eggs
- [ ] 1 bottle tomato sauce
- [ ] 1 bottle mayonnaise
- [ ] 2 bottles chutney
- [ ] 1 bottle vinegar
- [ ] 1 bottle soy sauce
- [ ] 1 bottle lemon juice
- [ ] 4 packets cream of mushroom soup powder
- [ ] 2 packets brown onion soup powder
- [ ] 1 packet meat stock cubes
- [ ] 2 kg rice
- [ ] 500 g spinach noodles
- [ ] 2 packets (500 g each) shell noodles
- [ ] 500 g crushed wheat or barley
- [ ] 2,5 kg sugar
- [ ] 1 kg cake flour
- [ ] 1 packet cornflour
- [ ] 500 g self-raising flour
- [ ] 1 can baking powder
- [ ] 1 container custard powder
- [ ] 1 small bottle vanilla essence
- [ ] 1 packet gelatine
- [ ] 250 g mixed dried fruit
- [ ] 250 g dried apricots
- [ ] 250 g seedless raisins
- [ ] 5 cans (185 g each) tuna
- [ ] 1 can (425 g) pilchards in tomato sauce
- [ ] 4 cans (410 g each) peas or 1,4 kg frozen peas
- [ ] 2 cans (225 g each) mixed vegetables
- [ ] 2 cans (410 g each) beans in tomato sauce
- [ ] 2 cans (450 g each) three-bean salad

- [ ] 2 bottles beetroot salad (omit if fresh beetroot is bought)
- [ ] 2 cans (115 g each) tomato paste
- [ ] 1 can (410 g) tomato and onion mix
- [ ] 2 cans (825 g each) pineapple pieces
- [ ] 1 can (825 g) sliced peaches in syrup
- [ ] 1 can (440 g) crushed pineapple
- [ ] 1 small can apricot jam
- [ ] 1 can (410 g) evaporated milk
- [ ] 1 can (397 g) condensed milk
- [ ] 3 packets jelly (1 pineapple flavour)
- [ ] 1 packet (250 g) crispbread
- [ ] 1 packet Tennis biscuits
- [ ] 1 packet marshmallows
- [ ] 150 ml sweet wine
- [ ] 15 ml brandy

Notes and birthdays

	MENU	FRESH PRODUCE
MON	Mince surprise*, carrot salad, beans in tomato sauce	*1 onion, carrots, 2 oranges (if desired for carrot salad)*
TUES	Bake-in-a-bag chicken*, spicy rice*, green beans, sweet pumpkin*	*Green beans, 1 onion, 750 g "boer" pumpkin or butternut*
WED	Rina's lasagne*, mixed salad	*2 onions, 1,25 litres milk, 100 g Cheddar cheese, vegetables for salad*
THURS	Baked fish fillets, chips, tomato salad*, sousboontjies	*6-8 potatoes, 3-4 tomatoes, 2 onions*
FRI	Bacon and banana toasts	*6 ripe bananas, 12-16 slices bread*
SAT	Braaied lamb chops, tropical potato salad*, beetroot salad, mixed salad	*5 large potatoes, beetroot (if preferred fresh), vegetables for salad*
SUN	Spanish chicken*, rice, mixed salad	*2 onions, 2 tomatoes, 3 carrots, vegetables for salad*
MON	Leftovers and cheese sauce surprise*	*6-8 rolls, 500 ml milk, 150 g Cheddar cheese*
TUES	Frikkadels*, fried potatoes, creamy squash*, peas	*2 slices white bread, 2 onions, 2 carrots, 6-8 potatoes, 2-3 large squash, cream (optional)*
WED	Chicken curry*, rice, sliced banana	*2 onions, 6 potatoes, 3 carrots, 4-6 bananas*
THURS	Grilled pork chops, mashed potatoes, squash, beans in tomato sauce	*6-8 potatoes, milk, 2-3 squash*
FRI	Pizza for Africa* (salami and mushrooms)	*250 g button mushrooms, 200 g Cheddar cheese, 200 g mozzarella cheese*
SAT	Sausage, fried eggs, sliced tomato, rolls	*2 tomatoes, 4-6 rolls*
SUN	Braaied chicken, roosterkoek*, coleslaw*, beetroot salad (Braai 4 extra halved chicken breasts to freeze for stir-fry chicken* later in the month)	*½ cabbage, beetroot (if preferred fresh), 1 pineapple, 2 bananas, milk*
MON	Cottage pie*, rice, green beans, sweet pumpkin *	*5 potatoes, 2 onions, milk, green beans, 750 g "boer" pumpkin or butternut*
TUES	Stir-fry chicken*, rice	*2 onions, cabbage, 3 carrots, 1 green pepper, 1 English cucumber*
WED	Grilled tuna and cheese rolls	*150 g Cheddar cheese, 6-8 bread rolls*

THURS	Festive pork chops*, peas, carrots, potatoes	*5-7 carrots, 6-8 potatoes*
FRI	Potato and onion delight*, mixed salad	*6 potatoes, 3 onions, 2 ripe tomatoes, 250 g button mushrooms, 1 apple, vegetables for salad*
SAT	Juicy chicken potjie*, rice	*3 onions, 3 carrots, green beans, 250 g young baby marrows, 10 small potatoes*
SUN	Melt-in-the-mouth steak*, rice, glazed sweet potatoes, green beans, beetroot salad	*4-5 sweet potatoes, green beans, beetroot (if preferred fresh)*
MON	Frikkadels*, yellow rice with raisins, peas, glazed carrots	*4-6 carrots*
TUES	Rina's lasagne*, mixed salad	*Vegetables for salad*
WED	Sausage, mashed potatoes, squash, beans in tomato sauce	*6-8 potatoes, milk, 2-3 squash*
THURS	Chicken in wine*, rice, peas, cauliflower with white sauce*	*Cauliflower, milk*
FRI	Hamburgers, chips	*Lettuce, 1 onion, 1 large tomato, 6-8 potatoes*
SAT	Macaroni cheese*, mixed salad	*2 ripe tomatoes, 150 g Cheddar cheese, 500 ml milk, vegetables for salad*
SUN	Coen's mince potjie*, mixed salad	*4 large onions, 250 g button mushrooms (optional), vegetables for salad*
MON	Fish lasagne*, mixed salad	*1 large onion, 500 ml milk, 100 g Cheddar cheese, vegetables for salad*
TUES	Lamb chops, sautéed potatoes, green beans, glazed sweet potatoes*	*6-8 potatoes, green beans, 4-5 sweet potatoes*
WED	Pizza for Africa* (bacon and mushrooms)	*250 g button mushrooms, 200 g Cheddar cheese, 200 g mozzarella cheese*

Desserts

Italian cream pudding*, jelly, custard	*1,5 litres milk*
Chocolate sponge pudding*	
Ice cream with chocolate sauce*	
Guava fridge tart*	*250 ml cream (optional)*
Creamy whip*, peaches, custard	*500 ml milk*
Catherine's cottage cheese tart*	*250 g smooth cottage cheese, 250 ml cream (optional)*

Shopping list

SPICES AND HERBS

- [ ] Salt
- [ ] Black pepper
- [ ] Cayenne pepper
- [ ] Curry powder
- [ ] Mixed spice
- [ ] Paprika
- [ ] Spice for rice
- [ ] Parsley
- [ ] 6 bay leaves
- [ ] Turmeric
- [ ] Nutmeg
- [ ] Ground cinnamon
- [ ] Flavour enhancer
- [ ] Ground ginger
- [ ] Garlic flakes

_____
_____
_____
_____
_____

MEAT AND FISH

- [ ] 1 whole chicken
- [ ] 4 packets (6-8 pieces each) chicken portions
- [ ] 1 packet (8-12 pieces) chicken portions
- [ ] 4 chicken breast halves
- [ ] 6 x 500 g mince
- [ ] 1 x 750 g mince
- [ ] 1 kg tenderise steak
- [ ] 1 packet (6-8 pieces) lamb chops
- [ ] 1 packet (8-12 pieces) lamb chops
- [ ] 2 packets (6-8 pieces each) pork chops
- [ ] 2 x sausage
- [ ] 6-8 hamburger patties
- [ ] 250 g sliced salami
- [ ] 4 x 250 g bacon
- [ ] 1 packet (800 g) fish fillets

_____
_____
_____
_____

GENERAL

- [ ] 800 g Cheddar cheese (omit if bought weekly – see fresh produce on menu)
- [ ] 400 g mozzarella cheese (omit if bought weekly – see fresh produce on menu)
- [ ] 250 g butter
- [ ] 1 kg margarine
- [ ] 1 litre ice cream (any flavour)
- [ ] 3 dozen eggs
- [ ] 1 bottle tomato sauce
- [ ] 1 bottle chutney
- [ ] 1 bottle vinegar
- [ ] 1 bottle Worcester sauce
- [ ] 2 bottles cooking oil
- [ ] 750 g mayonnaise
- [ ] 2 packets mushroom sauce powder
- [ ] 1 packet cream of mushroom soup powder
- [ ] 3 packets brown onion soup powder
- [ ] 1 packet thick vegetable soup powder
- [ ] 1 can (410 g) minestrone
- [ ] 1 can (410 g) cream of mushroom soup
- [ ] 1 can (410 g) tomato soup
- [ ] 1 chicken stock cube
- [ ] 3 kg rice
- [ ] 875 g spinach noodles
- [ ] 200 g macaroni
- [ ] 1 kg self-raising flour
- [ ] 1 kg bread flour
- [ ] 500 g cake flour
- [ ] 2 packets instant yeast
- [ ] 1 small can baking powder
- [ ] 2,5 kg sugar
- [ ] 1 packet brown sugar
- [ ] 1 container custard powder
- [ ] cream of tartar
- [ ] 1 can cocoa
- [ ] 250 g seedless raisins
- [ ] 4 cans (200 g each) tuna
- [ ] 1 can (410 g) ravioli
- [ ] 2 cans (115 g each) tomato paste
- [ ] 4 cans (410 g each) tomato and onion mix
- [ ] 2 small cans (225 g each) mixed vegetables

- [ ] 4 cans (410 g each) peas or 1,4 kg frozen peas
- [ ] 3 cans (420 g each) beans in tomato sauce
- [ ] 1 bottle sousboontjies
- [ ] 3 bottles beetroot salad (omit if fresh beetroot is bought)
- [ ] 1 can (425 g) crushed pineapple
- [ ] 1 can (440 g) pineapple pieces
- [ ] 2 cans (410 g each) sliced peaches
- [ ] 1 small can (225 g) apricots
- [ ] 1 large can (820 g) guavas
- [ ] 1 can (385 g) pears
- [ ] 1 can golden syrup
- [ ] 2 cans (410 g each) evaporated milk
- [ ] 1 can (397 g) condensed milk
- [ ] 1 packet lemon jelly powder
- [ ] 2 packets jelly powder (any kind)
- [ ] 2 packets red jelly powder
- [ ] 1 packet vanilla instant pudding
- [ ] 1 carton (250 ml) apricot juice
- [ ] 2 packets Tennis biscuits
- [ ] 2 packets Marie biscuits
- [ ] 1 medium cooking bag
- [ ] 375 ml dry white wine

Notes and birthdays

MENU	FRESH PRODUCE
MON Quick savoury tart*, carrot salad, beetroot salad	*500 ml milk, 100 g Cheddar cheese, carrots, 2 oranges (if desired for carrot salad), beetroot (if preferred fresh)*
TUES Agnes's noodles*, mixed salad	*1 onion, 1 green pepper, 1 tomato, 100 g Cheddar cheese, vegetables for salad*
WED Roast chicken, potatoes, pumpkin, green beans, carrot salad	*4-6 potatoes, pumpkin, green beans, carrots, 2 oranges (if desired for carrot salad)*
THURS Fish, mashed potatoes, peas, mixed salad	*4-6 potatoes, milk, vegetables for salad*
FRI Hamburgers, chips	*6-8 hamburger rolls, lettuce, onion, tomato, 6-8 potatoes*
SAT Aunt Marie's tuna tart*, potatoes, mixed salad, banana and bean salad*	*1 slice white bread, 250 ml milk, 1 onion, 4-6 potatoes, 3 bananas, vegetables for salad*
SUN Sherried chicken potjie*, rice, sliced banana	*3 carrots, 4 potatoes, 250 g button mushrooms, 3-5 bananas*
MON Fish with tartar sauce*, spinach, glazed carrots, mixed salad	*Milk, spinach, 4-6 carrots, vegetables for salad*
TUES Steak in wine*, potatoes, stir-fry vegetables	*4-6 potatoes*
WED Apricot chicken*, rice, broccoli, pumpkin, carrot salad	*Broccoli, pumpkin, carrots, 2 oranges (if desired for carrot salad)*
THURS Virginia's pork chops*, savoury rice*, green beans, mealies	*Green beans, mealies*
FRI Cheese, ham and tomato toasts	*Bread, cheese, tomato*
SAT Mavis's macaroni cheese*, mixed salad	*2 onions, 100 g Cheddar cheese, vegetables for salad*
SUN Braai (lamb chops, sausage), braai bread, mixed salad	*8-12 slices bread, cheese and tomato for braai bread, vegetables for salad*
MON Frikkadels*, mashed potatoes, marshmallow squash*, just carrots* (Frikkadels are not repeated later in the month, but double quantity anyway and use as needed)	*2 slices white bread, 2 onions, 7-8 carrots, 8-10 potatoes, milk, 3-4 squash*
TUES Aunt Minnie's tuna soufflé*, jacket potatoes, stir-fry vegetables, sliced pineapple	*1 large onion, 100 g Cheddar cheese, 250 ml milk, 4-6 potatoes, pineapple*

WED	Lasagne*, mixed salad	2 onions, 1 green pepper, 1 clove garlic, 500 ml milk, 80 g Cheddar cheese, vegetables for salad
THURS	Barcelona chicken*, yellow rice, carrots, green beans	2 onions, 4-6 carrots, green beans
FRI	All-time favourite beef rice, baby marrows with mushrooms*, carrot salad (Prepare Ina's salad delight* for Sunday)	500 g button mushrooms, 2 onions, 200 ml cream, 500 g baby marrows, carrots, 2 oranges (if desired for carrot salad)
SAT	Pizza for Africa* (pineapple and ham)	200 g Cheddar cheese, 200 g mozzarella cheese
SUN	Leg of lamb, roast potatoes, pumpkin, cauliflower with cheese, Ina's salad delight *	Potatoes, pumpkin, cauliflower, cheese, 1 onion, pineapple
MON	Quick savoury tart*, raw vegetable salad*, whole-wheat bread	500 ml milk, 100 g Cheddar cheese, 2 carrots, 125 g button mushrooms, cauliflower, tomatoes, baby marrow, green pepper, whole-wheat bread
TUES	Fish, stir-fried vegetables, tomato salad*	3-4 tomatoes, 2 onions
WED	Oxtail stew*, rice, green beans, stewed dried peaches	2 onions, 6 potatoes, green beans
THURS	Mince curry*, rice, sliced banana, tomato salad*	3 onions, 2 carrots, 1 green apple, 2 large potatoes, 4-6 bananas, 3-4 tomatoes
FRI	Quick cheese snacks*	250 g smooth cottage cheese, 8-10 slices rye bread, tomato (optional), 150 g Cheddar cheese
SAT	Sausage, mashed potatoes, beans in tomato sauce (hot)	4-6 potatoes, milk
SUN	Tipsy lamb potjie*, rice, bread rolls	2 onions, 4-6 potatoes, 250 g carrots, 250 g button mushrooms, 250 g baby marrows, bread rolls
MON	Leftovers (clean out refrigerator)	
TUES	Fried steak, jacket potatoes, spinach, carrots, mixed salad	4-6 potatoes, spinach, carrots, vegetables for salad

Desserts

Mum's melktert*	1 litre milk
Bananas with custard	500 ml milk, bananas
Ice cream with caramel sauce*	250 ml milk
Jelly snow* with custard	500 ml milk
Trifle *	1 trifle sponge, 250 ml cream, 1,25 litres milk
Apple tart with sultanas*	125 ml milk

Shopping list

SPICES AND HERBS

- [ ] Parsley
- [ ] Flavour enhancer
- [ ] Oregano
- [ ] Coarsely ground black pepper
- [ ] Basil
- [ ] Paprika
- [ ] Mild curry powder
- [ ] Garlic powder
- [ ] Mixed herbs
- [ ] Garlic salt
- [ ] Ground cinnamon
- [ ] Thyme
- [ ] Peri-peri
- [ ] Turmeric
- [ ] Ground coriander

_____
_____
_____
_____
_____
_____
_____
_____
_____

MEAT AND FISH

- [ ] 3 packets (6-8 pieces each) chicken portions
- [ ] 1 whole chicken
- [ ] 2 packets (4-6 pieces each) steak
- [ ] 6-8 pork chops
- [ ] 4-6 lamb chops
- [ ] 2 x sausage
- [ ] 1 kg tenderised steak
- [ ] 1 leg of lamb
- [ ] 1,25 kg oxtail, sliced
- [ ] 1,25 kg lamb knuckles
- [ ] 1 x 1 kg mince
- [ ] 1 x 750 g mince
- [ ] 1 x 500 g mince
- [ ] 3 x 800 g hake

- [ ] 250 g Vienna sausages
- [ ] 4 packets (250 g each) rindless bacon
- [ ] 1 packet hamburger patties
- [ ] 250 g garlic polony
- [ ] 450 g ham (any kind)

_____
_____
_____
_____
_____
_____
_____
_____
_____
_____

GENERAL

- [ ] 900 g Cheddar cheese (omit if bought weekly — see fresh produce on menu)
- [ ] 200 g mozzarella cheese (omit if bought weekly — see fresh produce on menu)
- [ ] 250 g smooth cottage cheese (omit if bought weekly — see fresh produce on menu)
- [ ] 1,5 kg margarine
- [ ] 1 kg frozen stir-fry vegetables
- [ ] 2 dozen eggs
- [ ] 1 bottle mayonnaise
- [ ] 2 bottles cooking oil
- [ ] 2 bottles chutney
- [ ] 1 bottle vinegar
- [ ] 1 bottle Worcester sauce
- [ ] 1 packet chicken stock cubes
- [ ] 1 packet brown onion soup powder
- [ ] 1 packet oxtail soup powder
- [ ] 2 packets cream of mushroom soup powder
- [ ] 2 kg rice
- [ ] 2,5 kg sugar
- [ ] 500 g spinach noodles
- [ ] 500 g shell noodles
- [ ] 500 g macaroni
- [ ] 2 x 500 g self-raising flour
- [ ] 1 kg cake flour

- [ ] 500 g crushed wheat or barley
- [ ] 250 g dried peaches
- [ ] 250 g seedless raisins
- [ ] 250 g sultanas
- [ ] 6 cans (185 g each) tuna
- [ ] 2 cans (300 g each) corned beef
- [ ] 2 cans (410 g each) peas or 700 g frozen peas
- [ ] 2 cans (410 g each) beans in tomato sauce
- [ ] 1 can (450 g) three-bean salad
- [ ] 1 can (410 g) tomato purée
- [ ] 2 cans (115 g each) tomato paste
- [ ] 1 can (410 g) tomato and onion mix
- [ ] 1 can (425 g) pineapple pieces
- [ ] 1 can (410 g) fruit salad
- [ ] 1 can (410 g) pie apples
- [ ] 5 packets jelly
- [ ] 1 bottle beetroot salad
- [ ] 1 bottle honey
- [ ] 1 jar sandwich spread
- [ ] 250 ml apricot juice
- [ ] 125 ml sherry
- [ ] 125 ml dry red wine
- [ ] 300 ml sweet wine
- [ ] 15 ml brandy

Notes and birthdays

MENU — FRESH PRODUCE

	MENU	FRESH PRODUCE
MON	Mince curry*, rice, sliced banana	1 onion, 2 carrots, 1 green apple, 2 large potatoes, 4-6 bananas
TUES	Apricot chicken*, rice, cauliflower with white sauce*, peas	Cauliflower, milk
WED	Frikkadels*, jacket potatoes, squash, carrot salad	2 slices white bread, 2 onions, 8 carrots, 6-8 potatoes, 100 ml milk, 2-3 squash, 2 oranges (if desired for carrot salad)
THURS	Chicken Tetrazzini*, mixed salad	2 onions, 250 g button mushrooms, 375 ml milk, 150 g Cheddar cheese, vegetables for salad
FRI	All-in-one soup*, cheese toasts (Prepare three-bean salad* for Sunday)	4 large carrots, 2 potatoes, 2 tomatoes, 3 onions, 150 g broccoli, 200 g cheese
SAT	Mince pancakes*, mixed salad Dessert: Sweet pancakes	750 ml milk, 1 onion, 100 g Cheddar cheese, vegetables for salad
SUN	Braaied lamb chops, rolls, three-bean salad*, Estelle's rice salad*	4-6 rolls, 2 onions, 2 green peppers, 1 tomato
MON	Cottage pie*, green beans, glazed sweet potatoes*, beetroot salad	5 potatoes, 1 onion, milk, green beans, 4-5 sweet potatoes, beetroot (if preferred fresh)
TUES	Fish cakes*, mashed potatoes, peas, beans in tomato sauce	1 onion, 6-7 potatoes, milk
WED	Potato and onion delight*, mixed salad	6 potatoes, 3 onions, 2 large ripe tomatoes, 250 g button mushrooms, 1 apple, vegetables for salad
THURS	Peach and late harvest chicken*, rice, boiled carrots, stir-fry (cabbage/onions/tomatoes)	4 onions, 4-6 carrots, cabbage, 2 ripe tomatoes
FRI	Pizza for Africa* (bacon and mushrooms)	200 g Cheddar cheese, 200 g mozzarella cheese, 250 g button mushrooms
SAT	Toasted sandwiches with versatile tuna filling*	12-16 slices bread, 1 onion, 1 tomato, 50 g Cheddar cheese
SUN	Melt-in-the-mouth steak*, rice, baby marrow stir-fry, orange sweet potatoes, peas	1 large onion, 1 ripe tomato, 400 g baby marrows, 4-5 sweet potatoes, 1 orange
MON	Fish lasagne*, mixed salad	1 onion, 500 ml milk, 100 g Cheddar cheese, vegetables for salad

Day	Meal	Ingredients
TUES	Lamb curry*, rice, stewed peaches	3 large onions, 1 green pepper, 4 carrots, 6 potatoes
WED	Sausage, mashed potatoes, squash, tomato salad*	6-8 potatoes, milk, 2-3 squash, 3 tomatoes, 2 onions
THURS	Chicken Tetrazzini*, mixed salad	Vegetables for salad
FRI	Cheese sauce surprise*	6-8 slices bread or rolls, 500 ml milk, 150 g Cheddar cheese
SAT	Fruity lamb potjie*, rice, stewed peaches	3 onions, 1 large ripe tomato, 250 g baby marrows, 6 potatoes, 250 g button mushrooms
SUN	Spanish chicken*, rice, mixed salad	2 onions, 2 tomatoes, 3 carrots, vegetables for salad
MON	Frikkadels*, mashed potatoes, sweet pumpkin*, green beans	1 onion, 5-7 potatoes, 200 ml milk, green beans, 750 g "boer" pumpkin or butternut
TUES	Hamburgers, chips	6-8 hamburger rolls, 1 tomato, lettuce, onion, 6-8 large potatoes
WED	Lamb chops, potatoes, carrots in orange sauce*, cauliflower, beetroot salad	4-6 potatoes, 5 carrots, 2 oranges, cauliflower, beetroot (if preferred fresh)
THURS	Bake-in-a-bag chicken*, spicy rice*, peas, mealies	
FRI	All-in-one soup, cheese and herb loaf*	100 g Cheddar cheese, 500 ml buttermilk
SAT	Rina's lasagne*, mixed salad	2 onions, 1,25 litres milk, 100 g Cheddar cheese, vegetables for salad
SUN	Braaied chicken (King Arthur's chicken marinade*), roosterkoek*, Rina's popular banana salad*, carrot salad, Estelle's rice salad*	2 onions, 5 bananas, 125 ml granadilla yoghurt, carrots, 1 green pepper, 1 tomato
MON	Smoorsnoek dish*, mixed salad	1 large onion, 1 lemon (optional), vegetables for salad
TUES	Chicken curry*, rice, sliced banana, tomato salad*	4 onions, 6 potatoes, 3 carrots, 4-6 bananas, 3-4 tomatoes
WED	Leftovers (clean out refrigerator)	

Desserts

Baked chocolate pudding*, custard	675 ml milk
Ice cream with caramel sauce*	250 ml milk
Lemon custard tart*	500 ml milk, 250 ml cream
Andriette's vinegar pudding with rum sauce*, ice cream	180 ml milk, 250 ml cream
Sago dumplings*	750 ml milk
Banana pudding*	875 ml milk, 5 ripe bananas

Shopping list

SPICES AND HERBS

- [ ] Salt
- [ ] Black pepper
- [ ] Cayenne pepper
- [ ] Curry powder
- [ ] Turmeric
- [ ] Ground cinnamon
- [ ] Basil
- [ ] Ground ginger
- [ ] Parsley
- [ ] Flavour enhancer
- [ ] Oregano
- [ ] Garlic flakes
- [ ] 5 bay leaves
- [ ] Ground cloves
- [ ] Paprika
- [ ] Mixed spice
- [ ] Spice for rice
- [ ] Nutmeg

_____

_____

_____

_____

_____

MEAT AND FISH

- [ ] 4 packets (6-8 pieces each) chicken portions
- [ ] 1 packet (8-12 pieces) chicken portions
- [ ] 2 whole chickens
- [ ] 1 packet (6-8 pieces) lamb chops
- [ ] 1 packet (8-12 pieces) lamb chops
- [ ] 1 kg tenderised steak
- [ ] 8-10 lamb neck chops
- [ ] 1 kg lamb shank, sliced
- [ ] 7 x 500 g mince
- [ ] 1 x sausage
- [ ] 6-8 hamburger patties
- [ ] 4 x 250 g shredded bacon

_____

_____

_____

_____

GENERAL

- [ ] 500 g Cheddar cheese (omit if bought weekly – see fresh produce on menu)
- [ ] 250 g butter
- [ ] 1,5 kg margarine
- [ ] 2 litres vanilla ice cream
- [ ] 3 dozen eggs
- [ ] 2 bottles cooking oil
- [ ] 1 bottle Worcester sauce
- [ ] 2 bottles chutney
- [ ] 1 bottle white vinegar
- [ ] 1 bottle tomato sauce
- [ ] 1 bottle medium-sweet mustard sauce
- [ ] 790 g mayonnaise
- [ ] 2 chicken stock cubes
- [ ] 1 beef stock cube
- [ ] 1 packet chicken marinade
- [ ] 2 packets mushroom sauce powder
- [ ] 1 packet brown onion soup powder
- [ ] 1 packet thick vegetable soup powder
- [ ] 4 packets cream of mushroom soup powder
- [ ] 1 packet oxtail soup powder
- [ ] 1 can (410 g) tomato soup
- [ ] 375 g split peas
- [ ] 3 kg rice
- [ ] 875 g spinach noodles
- [ ] 500 g shell noodles
- [ ] 1 kg bread flour
- [ ] 1,5 kg cake flour
- [ ] 1 packet cornflour
- [ ] 2 x 500 g self-raising flour
- [ ] 1 packet instant yeast
- [ ] 1 small can baking powder
- [ ] 1 container custard powder
- [ ] 1 packet sago
- [ ] 45 ml cocoa
- [ ] 1 packet bicarbonate of soda
- [ ] 1 small bottle vanilla essence
- [ ] 1 small bottle rum essence
- [ ] 2,5 kg sugar
- [ ] 150 ml brown sugar
- [ ] 250 g seedless raisins

- [ ] 1 kg dried peaches
- [ ] 250 g dried apricots
- [ ] 1 can (425 g) pilchards in tomato sauce
- [ ] 1 can (400 g) smoorsnoek
- [ ] 4 cans (200 g each) tuna
- [ ] 2 cans (410 g each) tomato and onion mix
- [ ] 2 cans (115 g each) tomato paste
- [ ] 1 small can (225 g) mixed vegetables
- [ ] 4 cans (410 g each) peas or 1,4 kg frozen peas
- [ ] 3 cans (420 g each) beans in tomato sauce
- [ ] 1 can (410 g) butter beans
- [ ] 1 can (230 g) sliced green beans
- [ ] 300 g frozen mealies
- [ ] 2 bottles beetroot salad (omit if bought fresh)
- [ ] 3 cans (410 g each) sliced peaches
- [ ] 1 small can apricot jam
- [ ] 1 can golden syrup
- [ ] 1 carton (250 ml) apricot juice
- [ ] 125 ml lemon juice
- [ ] 1 can (410 g) evaporated milk
- [ ] 2 cans (397 g each) condensed milk
- [ ] 1 packet Tennis biscuits
- [ ] 200 ml late harvest wine
- [ ] 1 medium baking bag

Notes and birthdays

MENU | FRESH PRODUCE

	MENU	FRESH PRODUCE
MON	Reeks's spaghetti bolognaise*, mixed salad	*2 onions, 1 green pepper, button mushrooms, vegetables for salad*
TUES	Sweet and tangy chicken*, bacon beans*, pumpkin, rice	*Green beans, pumpkin*
WED	Fish with tartar sauce*, chips, mixed salad, whole-wheat bread	*30 ml milk, 6-8 potatoes, vegetables for salad, whole-wheat bread*
THURS	Curry and rice*, tomato salad*, sliced banana	*Bananas, 4 onions, 3-4 tomatoes*
FRI	Virginia's pork chops*, roast potatoes, peas, carrots, mixed salad	*4-6 potatoes, 4-6 carrots, vegetables for salad*
SAT	Mavis's macaroni cheese*, mixed salad	*2 onions, 100 g Cheddar cheese, vegetables for salad*
SUN	Braai (lamb chops, sausage), braai bread, banana and bean salad*	*8-12 slices bread, cheese and tomato for braai bread, 3 bananas*
MON	Frikkadels*, rice, squash, broccoli, tomato salad* (Frikkadels are not repeated later in the month; double anyway and use as needed)	*2 slices white bread, 4 onions, 2 carrots, 2 potatoes, milk, 2-3 squash, broccoli, 3-4 tomatoes*
TUES	Baked asparagus fish*, savoury rice*, raw vegetable salad*	*500 ml milk, 100 g Cheddar cheese, 2 carrots, 125 g button mushrooms, cauliflower, 2 tomatoes, 125 g baby marrows, ½ green pepper*
WED	Fruity bobotie*, yellow rice, mixed salad	*2 slices brown bread, 200 ml milk, 2 onions, 1 green apple, vegetables for salad*
THURS	Farm soup*, whole-wheat bread	*4 carrots, 3 potatoes, 2 onions, 250 g cauliflower, celery, 2 cloves garlic, whole-wheat bread*
FRI	Hot dogs	*Long bread rolls*
SAT	Pasta à la Alrina*, mixed salad	*1 onion, 250 g button mushrooms, vegetables for salad*
SUN	Tipsy lamb potjie*, rice, bread rolls	*2 onions, 4-6 potatoes, 250 g carrots, 250 g button mushrooms, 250 g baby marrows, bread rolls*
MON	Mince curry*, rice, sliced banana, tomato salad* (Prepare Ina's salad delight* for Tuesday)	*3 onions, 2 carrots, 1 green apple, 2 potatoes, 3-4 tomatoes, bananas*
TUES	Steak in wine*, chips, Ina's salad delight*	*6-8 potatoes, 1 onion, pineapple*

Day	Meal	Ingredients
WED	Roast chicken, potatoes, Grandma Stella's pumpkin fritters*, green beans	*4-6 potatoes, pumpkin, green beans*
THURS	Reeks's spaghetti bolognaise*, mixed salad	*2 onions, 1 green pepper, button mushrooms, vegetables for salad*
FRI	Cathi Hempel's curried butternut soup*, bread rolls	*1,5 kg butternut, 1 onion, cream or sour cream (optional), bread rolls*
SAT	Cottage pie*, squash, beetroot salad	*5 potatoes, 1 onion, milk, 2-3 squash, beetroot (if preferred fresh)*
SUN	Leg of lamb, potato bake*, peas, carrots in orange sauce*	*6 potatoes, 250 ml cream, 5 large carrots, 1 orange*
MON	Fish cakes*, mashed potatoes, carrots, green beans	*1 onion, 4-6 potatoes, milk, 4-6 carrots, green beans*
TUES	Paprika lamb chops*, spinach, pumpkin, potatoes, carrot salad	*Spinach, pumpkin, 4-6 potatoes, 1 onion, 1 green pepper, carrots, 2 oranges (if desired for carrot salad)*
WED	Fruity bobotie*, yellow rice, mixed salad	*2 onions, 2 slices brown bread, 200 ml milk, 1 green apple, vegetables for salad*
THURS	Mum's bean soup*, bread rolls with cheese	*1 onion, bread rolls, cheese*
FRI	Fish, green beans, carrots, banana and bean salad*	*Green beans, 4-6 carrots, 3 bananas*
SAT	Mince curry* toasts	*1 onion, 2 carrots, 1 green apple, 2 large potatoes, 8-12 slices bread*
SUN	Braai (chicken portions), garlic bread*, tomato salad*, sousboontjies	*1 French loaf, 3-4 tomatoes, 2 onions*
MON	Leftovers (clean out refrigerator)	
TUES	Lamb chops, potatoes, green beans, carrots, mixed salad	*4-6 potatoes, green beans, 4-6 carrots, vegetables for salad*

Desserts

Mum's melktert*	*1 litre milk*
Stella's malva pudding*, custard	*750 ml milk*
Stewed peaches with custard	*500 ml milk*
Andriette's vinegar pudding with rum sauce*, ice cream	*180 ml milk, 250 ml cream*
Sago pudding*	*750 ml milk*
Baked apples with custard*	*6 red apples, 500 ml milk*

Shopping list

SPICES AND HERBS

- [ ] Oregano
- [ ] Garlic flakes
- [ ] Black pepper
- [ ] Paprika
- [ ] Flavour enhancer
- [ ] Garlic powder
- [ ] Masala
- [ ] Mild curry powder
- [ ] Ground cumin
- [ ] Garlic salt
- [ ] Parsley
- [ ] Cayenne pepper
- [ ] Turmeric
- [ ] Ground nutmeg

_____
_____
_____
_____

MEAT AND FISH

- [ ] 2 packets (6-8 pieces each) chicken portions
- [ ] 1 whole chicken
- [ ] 1 kg mince
- [ ] 6 x 500 g mince
- [ ] 750 g stewing beef or lamb
- [ ] 6-8 pork chops
- [ ] 2 packets (4-6 pieces each) lamb chops
- [ ] 1,25 kg lamb knuckles
- [ ] 6-8 lamb leg chops
- [ ] 500 g lamb shank
- [ ] 1 leg of lamb
- [ ] 1 x sausage
- [ ] 4-6 portions fillet of beef
- [ ] 3 x 800 g hake
- [ ] 6 packets (250 g each) rindless bacon
- [ ] 250 g Vienna sausages

_____
_____
_____
_____

GENERAL

- [ ] 300 g Cheddar cheese (omit if bought weekly – see fresh produce on menu)
- [ ] 1,5 kg margarine
- [ ] 1 litre ice cream
- [ ] 2 dozen eggs
- [ ] 1 bottle Worcester sauce
- [ ] 1 bottle vinegar
- [ ] 1 bottle lemon juice
- [ ] 1 bottle mayonnaise
- [ ] 1 bottle chutney
- [ ] 2 bottles cooking oil
- [ ] 1 packet oxtail soup powder
- [ ] 3 packets brown onion soup powder
- [ ] 2 packets cream of mushroom soup powder
- [ ] 1 packet sago
- [ ] 1 packet chicken stock cubes
- [ ] 2 packets (500 g each) spaghetti
- [ ] 500 g macaroni
- [ ] 500 g shell noodles
- [ ] 2 kg rice
- [ ] 2,5 kg sugar
- [ ] 1 kg cake flour
- [ ] 1 packet coconut
- [ ] 1 packet breadcrumbs
- [ ] 1 container custard powder
- [ ] 1 small bottle rum essence
- [ ] 500 g crushed wheat or barley
- [ ] 2 x 500 g brown sugar beans
- [ ] 250 g dried apricots
- [ ] 250 g sultanas
- [ ] 500 g dried peaches
- [ ] 2 cans (410 g each) peas or 700 g frozen peas
- [ ] 1 can (450 g) three-bean salad
- [ ] 1 can (225 g) mixed vegetables
- [ ] 2 cans (410 g each) beans in tomato sauce
- [ ] 1 can (410 g) asparagus
- [ ] 1 bottle beetroot salad
- [ ] 1 bottle sousboontjies
- [ ] 1 can (185 g) tuna
- [ ] 1 can (410 g) pilchards in tomato sauce
- [ ] 1 can (110 g) tomato paste

- [ ] 2 cans (410 g each) tomato purée
- [ ] 1 small can apricot jam
- [ ] 2 cans (410 g each) evaporated milk
- [ ] 250 ml orange juice
- [ ] 150 ml sweet wine
- [ ] 15 ml brandy
- [ ] 125 ml dry red wine

Notes and birthdays

	MENU	FRESH PRODUCE
MON	Spanish chicken*, rice, mixed salad	*2 onions, 2 tomatoes, 3 carrots, vegetables for salad*
TUES	Sausage, mashed potatoes, squash, peas	*6-8 potatoes, milk, 2-3 squash*
WED	Smoorsnoek dish*, mixed salad	*1 onion, 1 lemon (optional), vegetables for salad*
THURS	Cottage pie*, mealies, green beans, beetroot salad	*5 potatoes, 1 onion, milk, beetroot (if preferred fresh), green beans*
FRI	Pea soup*, cheese toasts	*1 onion, 1 carrot, 8-10 slices bread, 200 g cheese*
SAT	Mock venison*, rice, stewed fruit	
SUN	Braaied chicken (King Arthur's chicken marinade*), Estelle's rice salad*, mixed salad, potatoes in onion sauce*	*2 onions, 1 green pepper, 1 tomato, vegetables for salad, 6 large potatoes*
MON	Mince curry*, rice, sliced banana, tomato salad*	*3 onions, 2 carrots, 1 green apple, 2 large potatoes, 4-6 bananas, 3-4 tomatoes*
TUES	Tuna with noodles*, mixed salad	*150 g Cheddar cheese, 250 ml milk, vegetables for salad*
WED	Apricot chicken*, spicy rice*, green beans, sweet pumpkin*	*Green beans, 750 g "boer" pumpkin or butternut, 1 onion*
THURS	Frikkadels*, potatoes with parsley butter, glazed carrots, cauliflower	*2 slices white bread, 2 onions, 7-9 carrots, 100 ml milk, 8-10 potatoes, cauliflower*
FRI	Hamburgers, chips	*6-8 hamburger rolls, 6-8 large potatoes, 1 tomato, lettuce, 1 onion*
SAT	Sausage on the coals, braaied rolls with cheese and tomato, carrot salad	*6-8 rolls, 150 g Cheddar cheese, 2 tomatoes, carrots, 2 oranges (if desired for carrot salad)*
SUN	Melt-in-the-mouth steak*, rice, baby marrow stir-fry*, orange sweet potatoes*	*1 onion, 1 large ripe tomato, 400 g baby marrows, 4-5 sweet potatoes, 1 orange*
MON	Ask-for-more chicken*, rice, peas, carrots	*Carrots*
TUES	Macaroni cheese*, mixed salad	*2 ripe tomatoes, 150 g Cheddar cheese, 500 ml milk, vegetables for salad*
WED	Mock venison pie*, baked potatoes, stewed apples, green beans, beetroot salad	*125 ml milk, 4-6 potatoes, 4-6 green apples, green beans, beetroot (if preferred fresh)*

Day	Meal	Ingredients
THURS	Pea soup*, cheese toasts	*8-10 slices bread, 200 g Cheddar cheese*
FRI	Cheese sauce surprise*	*6-8 slices bread or rolls, 500 ml milk, 150 g Cheddar cheese*
SAT	Lamb curry*, rice, sliced banana, tomato salad*	*5 large onions, 1 green pepper, 4 carrots, 6 potatoes, 4-6 bananas, 3-4 tomatoes*
SUN	Chicken in wine*, yellow rice with raisins, peas, cauliflower with white sauce*, baked potatoes	*Cauliflower, milk, 4-6 potatoes*
MON	Fish cakes*, mashed potatoes, beans in tomato sauce, mixed salad	*1 onion, 5-7 potatoes, milk, vegetables for salad*
TUES	Spaghetti bolognaise*, mixed salad	*1 onion, 150 g Cheddar cheese, vegetables for salad*
WED	Baked pork chops, spicy rice*, cabbage, squash, stewed apples	*½ cabbage, 2-3 squash, 4-6 green apples*
THURS	Frikkadels*, rice, green beans, glazed sweet potatoes*	*Green beans, 4-5 sweet potatoes*
FRI	Bacon and banana toasts	*3-5 ripe bananas, 12-16 slices bread*
SAT	Braaied lamb chops, roosterkoek*, hot rice salad*, coleslaw*, mixed salad	*1 large onion, 125 g button mushrooms, ½ cabbage, 1 pineapple, 2 bananas, 25 ml milk, vegetables for salad*
SUN	Bake-in-a-bag chicken*, potatoes, glazed carrots, broccoli	*4-6 potatoes, carrots, broccoli*
MON	Leftovers (clean out refrigerator)	
TUES	Mince pancakes*, mixed salad	*750 ml milk, 1 onion, 100 g Cheddar cheese, vegetables for salad*
WED	Apricot chicken*, rice, peas, orange sweet potatoes*	*4-5 sweet potatoes, 1 orange*

Desserts

Dessert	Ingredients
Apple tart with sultanas*, cream	*125 ml milk, 250 ml cream*
Moira's pudding*	*1,25 litres milk*
Sago pudding*	*750 ml milk*
Quick ginger pudding*, custard	*500 ml milk*
Old-fashioned rice pudding*	*700 ml milk*
Honey cake*, cream	*125 ml milk, 250 ml cream*
Orange syrup cake*, ice cream	*200 ml milk, 4 oranges*

Shopping list

SPICES AND HERBS

- [ ] Salt
- [ ] Black pepper
- [ ] Cayenne pepper
- [ ] Parsley
- [ ] 5 bay leaves
- [ ] Flavour enhancer
- [ ] Nutmeg
- [ ] Mixed spice
- [ ] Paprika
- [ ] Celery salt
- [ ] 10 cloves
- [ ] Curry powder
- [ ] Turmeric
- [ ] Spice for rice
- [ ] Ground cinnamon
- [ ] Ground ginger
- [ ] Thyme
- [ ] Garlic flakes

_____

_____

_____

_____

MEAT AND FISH

- [ ] 5 packets (6-8 pieces each) chicken portions
- [ ] 1 packet (8-12 pieces) chicken portions
- [ ] 1 whole chicken
- [ ] 1 kg tenderised steak
- [ ] 2 kg stewing beef
- [ ] 8-10 lamb neck chops
- [ ] 8-12 lamb chops
- [ ] 100 g speck
- [ ] 250 g pork sausage
- [ ] 2 x sausage
- [ ] 6 x 500 g mince
- [ ] 6-8 hamburger patties
- [ ] 3 x 250 g diced bacon

_____

_____

_____

_____

GENERAL

- [ ] 800 g Cheddar cheese (omit if bought weekly – see fresh produce on menu)
- [ ] 1,5 kg margarine
- [ ] 250 g butter
- [ ] 1 litre vanilla ice cream
- [ ] 3 dozen eggs
- [ ] 2 bottles chutney
- [ ] 1 bottle vinegar
- [ ] 1 bottle Worcester sauce
- [ ] 1 bottle tomato sauce
- [ ] 2 bottles cooking oil
- [ ] 790 g mayonnaise
- [ ] 1 beef stock cube
- [ ] 1 packet chicken marinade
- [ ] 1 packet thick vegetable soup powder
- [ ] 1 packet oxtail soup powder
- [ ] 4 packets brown onion soup powder
- [ ] 5 packets cream of mushroom soup powder
- [ ] 3 kg rice
- [ ] 375 g split peas
- [ ] 250 g shell noodles
- [ ] 200 g macaroni
- [ ] 375 g spaghetti
- [ ] 2 kg cake flour
- [ ] 1 kg bread flour
- [ ] 500 g self-raising flour
- [ ] 1 packet instant yeast
- [ ] 1 small can baking powder
- [ ] 2,5 kg sugar
- [ ] 1 packet brown sugar
- [ ] 1 packet castor sugar
- [ ] 1 container custard powder
- [ ] 100 ml sago
- [ ] 1 small bottle vanilla essence
- [ ] 250 g sultanas
- [ ] 500 g mixed dried fruit
- [ ] 500 g seedless raisins
- [ ] 750 ml cornflakes
- [ ] 1 can (400 g) smoorsnoek
- [ ] 2 cans (198 g each) savoury light-meat tuna
- [ ] 1 can (200 g) tuna

- [ ] 1 can (425 g) pilchards in tomato sauce
- [ ] 1 small can (225 g) mixed vegetables
- [ ] 1 can (410 g) tomato purée
- [ ] 2 cans (410 g each) beans in tomato sauce
- [ ] 5 cans (410 g each) peas or 1,75 kg frozen peas
- [ ] 300 g frozen mealies
- [ ] 2 bottles beetroot (omit if bought fresh)
- [ ] 1 can (410 g) sliced peaches
- [ ] 1 can (385 g) pie apples
- [ ] 1 can (410 g) pears
- [ ] 1 small can apricot jam
- [ ] 1 can golden syrup
- [ ] 2 cartons (250 ml each) apricot juice
- [ ] 1 can (397 g) condensed milk
- [ ] 1 can (410 g) evaporated milk
- [ ] 2 packets ginger biscuits
- [ ] 1 medium baking bag
- [ ] 250 ml white wine

Notes and birthdays

August

	MENU	FRESH PRODUCE
MON	Lamb neck casserole*, cauliflower with cheese, pumpkin, rice, beetroot salad	*2 onions, cauliflower, Cheddar cheese, pumpkin, beetroot (if preferred fresh)*
TUES	Fish with tartar sauce*, chips, broccoli, sliced tomatoes	*6-8 potatoes, broccoli, 2 tomatoes, milk*
WED	All-time favourite beef*, rice, glazed sweet potatoes*, spinach, mixed salad	*200 ml cream, 250 g button mushrooms, 1 onion, 4-5 sweet potatoes, spinach, vegetables for salad*
THURS	Chicken Tetrazzini*, tomato salad*, sliced banana (Chicken Tetrazzini is not repeated later in the month; double anyway and use as needed)	*4 onions, 250 g button mushrooms, 375 ml milk, 150 g Cheddar cheese, 3-4 tomatoes, 4-5 bananas*
FRI	Sweet-and-sour pork*, rice, mixed salad	*Vegetables for salad, 1 green pepper*
SAT	Hamburgers, chips (Prepare Ina's salad delight* for Sunday)	*Hamburger rolls, 6-8 potatoes, lettuce, tomato, onion*
SUN	Braai (lamb rib, sausage), bread rolls, Ina's salad delight*	*Bread rolls, 1 onion, pineapple*
MON	Cathi Hempel's curried butternut soup*, bread rolls	*1,25 kg butternut, 1 onion, bread rolls*
TUES	Reeks's spaghetti bolognaise*, sliced pineapple, sliced tomato	*2 onions, 1 green pepper, button mushrooms, pineapple, 2 tomatoes*
WED	Fish, mashed potatoes, peas, beans in tomato sauce (hot)	*4-6 potatoes, milk*
THURS	Roast chicken, savoury rice*, Grandma Stella's pumpkin fritters*, cauliflower with cheese	*Pumpkin, cauliflower, Cheddar cheese*
FRI	Lasagne*, mixed salad	*2 onions, 1 green pepper, 1 clove garlic, 500 ml milk, 80 g Cheddar cheese, vegetables for salad*
SAT	Mavis's macaroni cheese*, mixed salad	*2 onions, 100 g Cheddar cheese, vegetables for salad*
SUN	Barcelona chicken*, roast potatoes, green beans, marshmallow squash*	*2 onions, 4-6 potatoes, green beans, 3-4 squash*
MON	Pizza for Africa* (bacon and mushrooms)	*200 g Cheddar cheese, 200 g mozzarella cheese, 250 g button mushrooms*
TUES	Steak in wine*, jacket potatoes, stir-fried vegetables	*4-6 potatoes*
WED	Sweet and tangy chicken*, pumpkin, peas, rice, mixed salad	*Pumpkin, vegetables for salad*

Day	Meal	Ingredients
THURS	Farm soup*, bread rolls	Celery, 2 cloves garlic, 4 carrots, 3 potatoes, 2 onions, 250 g cauliflower
FRI	Baked asparagus fish*, chips, broccoli, carrots	6-8 potatoes, broccoli, 4-6 carrots, 100 g Cheddar cheese, 500 ml milk
SAT	Quick cheese snacks *	8-10 slices rye bread, 250 g smooth cottage cheese, 100 g Cheddar cheese, tomato (optional)
SUN	Roast leg of pork, apple sauce, potato bake*, peas, carrots in orange sauce*	6 potatoes, 250 ml cream, 5 large carrots, 1 orange
MON	Oxtail stew*, rice, carrots, green beans, mixed salad	6 potatoes, 4-6 carrots, green beans, 2 onions, vegetables for salad
TUES	Fish, chips, bacon beans*, mealies, mixed salad	6-8 potatoes, green beans, mealies, vegetables for salad
WED	Lasagne*, mixed salad	2 onions, 1 green pepper, 1 clove garlic, 500 ml milk, 80 g Cheddar cheese, vegetables for salad
THURS	Chicken à la Madelein*, mixed salad	2 carrots, 1 onion, 125 g button mushrooms, 1 green pepper, 250 ml cream, vegetables for salad
FRI	Sausage, eggs, jacket potatoes, beans in tomato sauce (Prepare Ina's salad delight* for Sunday)	4-6 potatoes
SAT	Frikkadels*, rice, stir-fried vegetables (Frikkadels aren't repeated later in the month; double anyway and use as needed)	2 slices white bread, 2 onions, 2 carrots, 2 potatoes, 100 ml milk
SUN	Braai (lamb chops, sausage), bread rolls, Ina's salad delight*	Bread rolls, 1 onion, pineapple
MON	Quick savoury tart*, carrot salad, mixed salad	Carrots, 2 oranges (if desired for carrot salad), 100 g Cheddar cheese, 500 ml milk
TUES	Leftovers (clean out refrigerator)	
WED	Fish with tartar sauce*, carrots, peas, squash, mixed salad	4-6 carrots, 2-3 squash, vegetables for salad, milk

Desserts

Stella's malva pudding*, custard	750 ml milk
Stewed peaches with custard	500 ml milk
Bananas with custard	500 ml milk
Quick pudding*	250 ml milk
Apple tart with sultanas*, cream	125 ml milk, 250 ml cream
Strawberry pudding*	

Shopping list

SPICES AND HERBS

- [ ] Flavour enhancer
- [ ] Black pepper
- [ ] Garlic powder
- [ ] Coarsely ground black pepper
- [ ] Paprika
- [ ] Peri-peri
- [ ] Oregano
- [ ] Mild curry powder
- [ ] Garlic flakes
- [ ] Mixed herbs
- [ ] Thyme

_____
_____
_____
_____

MEAT AND FISH

- [ ] 1,25 kg lamb neck chops
- [ ] 1 kg lamb rib
- [ ] 4-6 lamb chops
- [ ] 3 x 500 g mince
- [ ] 2 x 750 g mince
- [ ] 1 kg tenderised steak
- [ ] 4-6 pieces fillet of beef
- [ ] 1,25 kg oxtail
- [ ] 750 g pork fillet, cubed
- [ ] 1 leg of pork
- [ ] 3 x sausage
- [ ] 3 whole chickens
- [ ] 2 packets (6-8 pieces each) chicken portions
- [ ] 5 x 800 g hake
- [ ] 5 packets (250 g each) rindless bacon
- [ ] 1 packet hamburger patties
- [ ] 250 g garlic polony
- [ ] 500 g Vienna sausages
- [ ] 150 g ham or salami, sliced (any kind)

_____
_____
_____
_____

GENERAL

- [ ] 850 g Cheddar cheese (omit if bought weekly — see fresh produce on menu)
- [ ] 200 g mozzarella cheese (omit if bought weekly — see fresh produce on menu)
- [ ] 250 g smooth cottage cheese (omit if bought weekly — see fresh produce on menu)
- [ ] 2 dozen eggs
- [ ] 1,5 kg margarine
- [ ] 1 packet frozen stir-fry vegetables
- [ ] 2 bottles cooking oil
- [ ] 1 bottle mayonnaise
- [ ] 1 bottle chutney
- [ ] 1 bottle tomato sauce
- [ ] 1 small bottle Worcester sauce
- [ ] 1 small bottle soy sauce
- [ ] 1 packet meat stock cubes
- [ ] 1 packet chicken stock cubes
- [ ] 2 packets cream of mushroom soup powder
- [ ] 1 packet brown onion soup powder
- [ ] 1 packet oxtail soup powder
- [ ] 500 g shell noodles
- [ ] 500 g spaghetti
- [ ] 2 packets (500 g each) spinach noodles
- [ ] 2,5 kg sugar
- [ ] 2 kg rice
- [ ] 2 kg cake flour
- [ ] 1 packet cornflour
- [ ] 500 g self-raising flour
- [ ] 1 packet breadcrumbs
- [ ] 1 packet bicarbonate of soda
- [ ] 1 container custard powder
- [ ] 1 small bottle vanilla essence
- [ ] 250 g dried apricots
- [ ] 250 g seedless raisins
- [ ] 500 g dried peaches
- [ ] 500 g sugar beans
- [ ] 2 packets crushed wheat or barley
- [ ] 1 can (300 g) corned beef
- [ ] 2 cans (410 g each) tomato purée
- [ ] 4 cans (115 g each) tomato paste
- [ ] 1 can (410 g) tomato and onion mix

- [ ] 5 cans (410 g each) peas or 1,75 kg frozen peas
- [ ] 1 bottle beetroot (omit if bought fresh)
- [ ] 1 can (410 g) asparagus
- [ ] 2 cans (450 g each) three-bean salad
- [ ] 2 cans (410 g each) beans in tomato sauce
- [ ] 1 can (825 g) pineapple pieces
- [ ] 1 small can apricot jam
- [ ] 1 small can strawberry jam
- [ ] 1 can (410 g) pie apples
- [ ] 1 small bottle honey
- [ ] 3 cans (410 g each) evaporated milk
- [ ] 1 jar apple sauce
- [ ] 1 packet strawberry jelly powder
- [ ] 2 x 250 ml orange juice
- [ ] 125 ml dry red wine
- [ ] 45 ml sherry

Notes and birthdays

	MENU	FRESH PRODUCE
MON	Chicken stew*, mixed salad	*2 onions, 4 ripe tomatoes, 250 g Cheddar cheese, vegetables for salad*
TUES	Fish cakes*, mashed potatoes, squash, peas	*1 onion, 5-7 potatoes, 200 ml milk, 2-3 squash*
WED	Frikkadels*, rice, green beans, pumpkin	*2 slices white bread, 2 onions, 2 carrots, 2 potatoes, 100 ml milk, green beans, "boer" pumpkin or butternut*
THURS	Lamb curry*, rice, sliced banana	*3 onions, 1 green pepper, 4 carrots, 6 potatoes, 4-6 bananas*
FRI	Pizza for Africa* (pineapple and ham)	*200 g Cheddar cheese, 200 g mozzarella cheese*
SAT	Braaied chicken (King Arthur's chicken marinade*) tropical potato salad*, carrot salad, garlic rolls*	*1 onion, 5 large potatoes, carrots, 2 oranges (if desired for carrot salad), 4-6 long rolls*
SUN	Bobotie*, yellow rice with raisins, peas, stewed dried fruit	*5 onions, 2 slices white bread, 375 ml milk*
MON	Tomato mince*, mixed salad, carrot salad	*1 onion, 100 g Cheddar cheese, vegetables for salad, carrots, 2 oranges (if desired for carrot salad)*
TUES	Smoorsnoek dish*, mixed salad	*1 large onion, 1 lemon (optional), vegetables for salad*
WED	Cheesy potatoes*, sliced pineapple, sliced tomato, carrot salad	*4-6 potatoes, 500 ml milk, 100 g Cheddar cheese, 1 pineapple, 2 tomatoes, carrots, 2 oranges (if desired for carrot salad)*
THURS	Pot-roast lamb chops with potatoes, glazed sweet potatoes*, green beans	*5-7 potatoes, 4-5 sweet potatoes, green beans*
FRI	Cheese sauce surprise*	*6-8 slices bread or rolls, 500 ml milk, 150 g Cheddar cheese*
SAT	Sausage on the coals, roosterkoek*, quick bean salad*, sliced tomatoes	*1 onion, 2 tomatoes*
SUN	Bake-in-a-bag chicken*, rice baby marrow stir-fry*, glazed carrots, peas	*1 large onion, 1 large ripe tomato, 400 g baby marrows, 5-7 carrots*
MON	Toasted sandwiches with versatile tuna filling*	*12-16 slices bread, 1 onion, 1 tomato, 50 g Cheddar cheese*

Day	Meal	Ingredients
TUES	Chicken Tetrazzini*, mixed salad	2 onions, 250 g button mushrooms, 375 ml milk, 150 g Cheddar cheese, vegetables for salad
WED	Russian sausages, fried eggs, creamstyle sweetcorn, rolls	4-6 bread rolls
THURS	Apricot chicken*, rice, peas, carrot salad	Carrots, 2 oranges (if desired for carrot salad)
FRI	Fish lasagne*, mixed salad	1 large onion, 500 ml milk, 100 g Cheddar cheese, vegetables for salad
SAT	Braaied lamb chops, tomato and onion toasts, Estelle's rice salad*, mixed salad	3 tomatoes, 8-12 slices bread, 2 onions, 1 green pepper, vegetables for salad
SUN	Frikkadels*, potatoes, squash, cauliflower with white sauce*, glazed sweet potatoes*	4-6 potatoes, 2-3 squash, cauliflower, milk, 4-5 sweet potatoes
MON	Leftovers (clean out refrigerator)	
TUES	Spaghetti bolognaise*, mixed salad	1 onion, 200 g Cheddar cheese, vegetables for salad
WED	Baked pork chops, spicy rice*, stewed apples, peas	4-6 green apples
THURS	Tuna with noodles*, mixed salad	150 g Cheddar cheese, 250 ml milk, vegetables for salad
FRI	Cottage pie*, cauliflower, sweet pumpkin* (Prepare three-bean salad* for Sunday)	5 potatoes, 2 onions, milk, cauliflower, 750 g ripe "boer" pumpkin or butternut
SAT	Chicken à la King*, rice, sliced tomato, sliced cucumber	2 onions, 1 green pepper, 4 tomatoes, 700 ml milk, cucumber
SUN	Steak over the coals, three-bean salad*, beetroot, carrot salad	1 onion, 1 green pepper, beetroot (if preferred fresh), carrots, 2 oranges (if desired for carrot salad)
MON	Hamburgers and chips	6-8 hamburger rolls, 1 onion, 1 tomato, lettuce, 6-8 large potatoes
TUES	Chicken Tetrazzini*, mixed salad	Vegetables for salad

Desserts

Dessert	Ingredients
Creamy whip*, custard	500 ml milk
Quick banana dessert*	6 ripe bananas, 500 ml milk
Granadilla fridge tart*	350 ml granadilla yoghurt, 125 ml cream
Ice-cream surprise*	4 ripe, firm bananas, 250 ml cream, meringues
Chocolate peaches*, cream	125 ml cream
Moira's pudding*	1,25 litres milk

Shopping list

SPICES AND HERBS

- [ ] Salt
- [ ] Black pepper
- [ ] Cayenne pepper
- [ ] Parsley
- [ ] Ground cinnamon
- [ ] Curry powder
- [ ] Ground ginger
- [ ] Turmeric
- [ ] 7 bay leaves
- [ ] Oregano
- [ ] Garlic powder
- [ ] Flavour enhancer
- [ ] Mixed herbs
- [ ] Paprika
- [ ] Mixed spice
- [ ] Garlic flakes
- [ ] Thyme
- [ ] Spice for rice
- [ ] Nutmeg
- [ ] Basil

_____

_____

MEAT AND FISH

- [ ] 4 whole chickens
- [ ] 2 packets (8-12 pieces each) chicken portions
- [ ] 1 packet (6-8 pieces) chicken portions
- [ ] 7 x 500 g mince
- [ ] 1 x sausage
- [ ] 4-6 steaks (own choice)
- [ ] 8-10 lamb neck chops
- [ ] 1 packet (6-8 pieces) lamb chops
- [ ] 1 packet (8-12 pieces) lamb chops
- [ ] 6-8 pork chops
- [ ] 250 g ham (any kind)
- [ ] 6-8 Russian sausages
- [ ] 2 x 250 g bacon
- [ ] 6-8 hamburger patties

_____

_____

_____

GENERAL

- [ ] 1,2 kg Cheddar cheese (omit if bought weekly – see fresh produce on menu)
- [ ] 200 g mozzarella cheese (omit if bought weekly – see fresh produce on menu)
- [ ] 1,5 kg margarine
- [ ] 250 g butter
- [ ] 1 litre vanilla ice cream
- [ ] 3 dozen eggs
- [ ] 2 bottles chutney
- [ ] 1 bottle vinegar
- [ ] 1 bottle tomato sauce
- [ ] 1 bottle Worcester sauce
- [ ] 2 bottles cooking oil
- [ ] 1 bottle (790 g) mayonnaise
- [ ] 1 chicken stock cube
- [ ] 1 packet chicken marinade
- [ ] 1 packet cream of chicken soup powder
- [ ] 6 packets cream of mushroom soup powder
- [ ] 1 packet oxtail soup powder
- [ ] 1 packet brown onion soup powder
- [ ] 1 can (410 g) tomato soup
- [ ] 3 kg rice
- [ ] 1 packet macaroni
- [ ] 375 g spaghetti
- [ ] 2 x 500 g shell noodles
- [ ] 375 g spinach noodles
- [ ] 1 kg cake flour
- [ ] 1 kg self-raising flour
- [ ] 1 kg white bread flour
- [ ] 1 packet instant yeast
- [ ] 1 can baking powder
- [ ] 2,5 kg sugar
- [ ] 30 ml soft brown sugar
- [ ] 1 packet castor sugar
- [ ] 1 container custard powder
- [ ] 1 packet gelatine
- [ ] 1 packet corn flakes
- [ ] 250 g seedless raisins
- [ ] 500 g mixed dried fruit
- [ ] 1 can (425 g) pilchards in tomato sauce
- [ ] 4 cans (200 g each) tuna

- [ ] 2 cans (198 g each) savoury light-meat tuna
- [ ] 1 can (400 g) smoorsnoek
- [ ] 1 can (225 g) mixed vegetables
- [ ] 5 cans (410 g each) peas or 1,75 kg frozen peas
- [ ] 1 can (410 g) creamstyle sweetcorn
- [ ] 3 cans (420 g each) beans in tomato sauce
- [ ] 1 can (410 g) butter beans
- [ ] 1 can (230 g) sliced green beans
- [ ] 1 bottle beetroot (omit if bought fresh)
- [ ] 2 cans (410 g each) tomato and onion mix
- [ ] 1 can (410 g) tomato purée
- [ ] 1 can (65 g) tomato paste
- [ ] 1 can (425 g) pineapple pieces
- [ ] 1 can (425 g) crushed pineapple
- [ ] 1 small can (225 g) sliced peaches
- [ ] 1 can (820 g) peach halves
- [ ] 1 can (115 g) granadilla pulp
- [ ] 1 small can apricot jam
- [ ] 1 can golden syrup
- [ ] 1 carton (250 ml) apricot juice
- [ ] 30 ml lemon juice
- [ ] 15 ml condensed milk
- [ ] 2 cans (410 g each) evaporated milk
- [ ] 1 packet granadilla or lemon jelly powder
- [ ] 1 packet jelly powder (any flavour)
- [ ] ½ packet Tennis biscuits
- [ ] 1 packet Choc Crust biscuits
- [ ] 1 Peppermint Crisp
- [ ] 10 ml brandy or sherry

Notes and birthdays

	MENU	FRESH PRODUCE
MON	Baked pork chops, potatoes in onion sauce*, carrots, broccoli	*6 large potatoes, 4-6 carrots, broccoli*
TUES	Tipsy lamb potjie*, rice, mixed salad	*2 onions, 4-6 potatoes, 250 g carrots, 250 g button mushrooms, 250 g baby marrows, vegetables for salad*
WED	Frikkadels*, mashed potatoes, marshmallow squash*, spinach, beetroot salad	*2 onions, 2 carrots, 2 potatoes, 2 slices white bread, 100 ml milk, 3-4 squash, spinach, beetroot (if preferred fresh)*
THURS	Fish cakes*, peas, carrots, mixed salad	*1 onion, 4-6 carrots, vegetables for salad*
FRI	Sherried chicken potjie*, rice, carrot salad	*3 carrots, 4 potatoes, 250 g button mushrooms, carrots for salad, 2 oranges (if desired for carrot salad)*
SAT	Sausage, potato bake*, mixed salad	*6 potatoes, 250 ml cream, vegetables for salad*
SUN	Braai (chicken portions), garlic bread*, banana and bean salad*	*French loaf, 3 bananas*
MON	Sweet-and-sour pork*, rice, mixed salad	*1 green pepper, vegetables for salad*
TUES	Barcelona chicken*, carrots, spinach, savoury rice*	*2 onions, 4-6 carrots, spinach*
WED	Fish with tartar sauce*, stir-fried vegetables, carrot salad	*Milk, carrots, 2 oranges (if desired for carrot salad)*
THURS	Fruity bobotie*, yellow rice, mixed salad	*2 onions, 2 slices brown bread, 200 ml milk, 1 green apple, vegetables for salad*
FRI	Pizza for Africa* (salami and mushrooms)	*200 g Cheddar cheese, 200 g mozzarella cheese, 250 g button mushrooms*
SAT	Tuna salad*, whole-wheat crispbread with cheese	*Pineapple, 1 large tomato, lettuce, Cheddar cheese*
SUN	Braai (lamb rib, sausage), jacket potatoes, carrot salad	*4-6 potatoes, carrots, 2 oranges (if desired for carrot salad)*
MON	Quick cheese snacks*, mixed salad	*8-10 slices rye bread, 150 g Cheddar cheese, 250 g smooth cottage cheese, vegetables for salad*
TUES	Steak in wine*, jacket potatoes, mixed salad	*4-6 potatoes, vegetables for salad*
WED	Cape pear chicken*, potato bake*, cauliflower with cheese, carrots	*6 potatoes, 250 ml cream, cauliflower, Cheddar cheese, 4-6 carrots*

THURS	Eric's mock crayfish*, whole-wheat crispbread, mixed salad	*1 onion, 25 ml milk, vegetables for salad*
FRI	Hamburgers, chips (Prepare Ina's salad delight* for Sunday)	*Hamburger rolls, lettuce, onion, tomato, 6-8 potatoes*
SAT	Braai (chicken portions), carrot salad, beetroot salad, bread rolls	*Carrots, 2 oranges (if desired for carrot salad), bread rolls, beetroot (if preferred fresh)*
SUN	Cold meats, Ina's salad delight*, potato salad, whole-wheat bread	*Cold meats, 1 onion, pineapple, 4-5 potatoes, whole-wheat bread*
MON	Chicken à la Madelein*, mixed salad	*2 carrots, 1 onion, 125 g button mushrooms, 1 green pepper, 250 ml cream, vegetables for salad*
TUES	Agnes's noodles*, carrot salad, garlic bread*	*1 onion, 1 green pepper, 1 tomato, 100 g Cheddar cheese, carrots, 2 oranges (if desired for carrot salad), French loaf*
WED	Fish (cold), rice salad*, mixed salad, whole-wheat bread	*3 bananas, 1 green pepper, pineapple, 1 tomato, parsley (optional), vegetables for salad, whole-wheat bread*
THURS	Paprika lamb chops*, bacon beans*, rice mealies	*1 onion, 1 green pepper, green beans, mealies*
FRI	Mavis's macaroni cheese*, sliced tomatoes, sliced pineapple	*2 onions, 100 g Cheddar cheese, 2 tomatoes, pineapple*
SAT	Frikkadels*, mashed potatoes, squash, carrots	*4-6 potatoes, 100 ml milk, 2-3 squash, 4-6 carrots*
SUN	Braai (lamb chops, sausage), braai bread, beetroot salad, sousboontjies	*8-12 slices bread, cheese, tomato, beetroot (if preferred fresh)*
MON	Leftovers (clean out refrigerator)	
TUES	Aunt Marie's tuna tart*, mixed salad	*1 slice white bread, 250 ml milk, 1 onion, vegetables for salad*
WED	Reeks's spaghetti bolognaise*, raw vegetable salad*	*2 onions, 2 green peppers, 250 g button mushrooms, 250 ml each carrots, cauliflower, tomatoes, baby marrows*

Desserts

Quick pudding*	*250 ml milk*
Baked apples*	*4-6 red apples*
Ice cream with chocolate sauce*	
Instant pudding, canned peaches	*500 ml milk*
Jelly custard*, with custard	*500 ml milk*
Fruit salad	*Fruit*

Shopping list

SPICES AND HERBS

- [ ] Parsley
- [ ] Flavour enhancer
- [ ] Black pepper
- [ ] Ground coriander
- [ ] Salt
- [ ] Mild curry powder
- [ ] Garlic powder
- [ ] Mixed herbs
- [ ] Turmeric
- [ ] Ground ginger
- [ ] Cloves
- [ ] Ground cinnamon
- [ ] Cinnamon sticks

_____

_____

_____

MEAT AND FISH

- [ ] 1,25 kg lamb knuckles
- [ ] 6-8 lamb leg chops
- [ ] 4-6 lamb chops
- [ ] 750 g lamb rib
- [ ] 2 x 1 kg mince
- [ ] 2 x 500 g mince
- [ ] 4-6 pork chops
- [ ] 750 g pork fillet, cubed
- [ ] 4-6 pieces fillet of beef
- [ ] 3 x sausage
- [ ] 1 whole chicken
- [ ] 5 packets (6-8 pieces each) chicken portions
- [ ] 3 x 800 g hake
- [ ] 4 packets (250 g each) rindless bacon
- [ ] 250 g garlic polony
- [ ] 200 g salami
- [ ] 150 g ham or salami
- [ ] 500 g cold meats (own choice)
- [ ] 1 packet hamburger patties

_____

_____

_____

_____

GENERAL

- [ ] 500 g Cheddar cheese (omit if bought weekly – see fresh produce on menu)
- [ ] 250 g smooth cottage cheese (omit if bought weekly – see fresh produce on menu)
- [ ] 1,5 kg margarine
- [ ] 1 litre vanilla ice cream
- [ ] 2 dozen eggs
- [ ] 1 packet stir-fry vegetables
- [ ] 1 bottle vinegar
- [ ] 1 bottle mayonnaise
- [ ] 1 bottle tomato sauce
- [ ] 2 bottles cooking oil
- [ ] 1 small bottle Worcester sauce
- [ ] 1 small bottle soy sauce
- [ ] 1 bottle chutney
- [ ] 1 small bottle lemon juice
- [ ] 1 small bottle Tabasco sauce
- [ ] 3 packets brown onion soup powder
- [ ] 2 packets oxtail soup powder
- [ ] 1 packet cream of mushroom soup powder
- [ ] 500 g shell noodles
- [ ] 500 g macaroni
- [ ] 500 g spaghetti
- [ ] 1 kg cake flour
- [ ] 1 packet cornflour
- [ ] 500 g self-raising flour
- [ ] Cream of tartar
- [ ] 1 small bottle vanilla essence
- [ ] 1 can baking powder
- [ ] 1 can cocoa
- [ ] 1 container custard powder
- [ ] 1 packet chicken stock cubes
- [ ] 2 kg rice
- [ ] 2,5 kg sugar
- [ ] 250 g dried apricots
- [ ] 250 g seedless raisins
- [ ] 7 cans (185 g each) tuna
- [ ] 1 can (425 g) pilchards in tomato sauce
- [ ] 2 cans (425 g each) tomato purée
- [ ] 1 can (425 g) tomato and onion mix
- [ ] 1 can (425 g) beans in tomato sauce

- [ ] 1 can (425 g) peas or 350 g frozen peas
- [ ] 1 can (450 g) three-bean salad
- [ ] 1 bottle sousboontjies
- [ ] 2 bottles beetroot salad
- [ ] 1 can (825 g) pineapple pieces
- [ ] 1 can (410 g) evaporated milk
- [ ] 1 small jar sandwich spread
- [ ] 2 packets instant pudding
- [ ] 1 packet jelly powder
- [ ] 1 packet marshmallows
- [ ] 250 ml pear juice
- [ ] 150 ml sweet wine
- [ ] 15 ml brandy
- [ ] 175 ml sherry
- [ ] 125 ml dry red wine

Notes and birthdays

November

	MENU	FRESH PRODUCE
MON	Tuna salad*, whole-wheat crispbread with cheese	*Pineapple, 1 tomato, lettuce, Cheddar cheese*
TUES	Barcelona chicken*, rice, marshmallow squash*, carrots	*2 onions, 3-4 squash, 4-6 carrots*
WED	Lasagne*, mixed salad	*2 onions, 1 green pepper, 1 clove garlic, 500 ml milk, 80 g Cheddar cheese, vegetables for salad*
THURS	Sausage, mashed potatoes, peas, carrots	*Potatoes, milk, 4-6 carrots*
FRI	Sherried chicken potjie*, rice, mixed salad	*3 carrots, 4 potatoes, 250 g button mushrooms, vegetables for salad*
SAT	Mince toasts	*8-12 slices bread*
SUN	Braai (pork chops, sausage), garlic bread*, mixed salad	*1 French loaf, vegetables for salad*
MON	Fish (cold), beans in tomato sauce, creamstyle sweet-corn, sliced pineapple	*1 pineapple*
TUES	Pizza for Africa* (pineapple and ham)	*200 g Cheddar cheese, 200 g mozzarella cheese*
WED	Frikkadels* (cold), jacket potatoes (cold), carrot salad, sliced tomatoes, beans in tomato sauce	*2 slices white bread, 2 onions, 2 carrots, 6-8 potatoes, 2 tomatoes, carrots, 2 oranges (if desired in carrot salad)*
THURS	Grilled lamb chops, potato bake*, pumpkin, mixed salad	*6 potatoes, 250 ml cream, pumpkin, vegetables for salad*
FRI	Fish (cold), mixed salad, whole-wheat bread	*Vegetables for salad, whole-wheat bread*
SAT	Hot dogs, chips	*Bread rolls, 6-8 potatoes*
SUN	Steak over the coals, jacket potatoes, mixed salad	*4-6 potatoes, vegetables for salad*
MON	Reeks's spaghetti bolognaise*, peas, mixed salad (prepare Ina's salad delight* for Tuesday)	*1 green pepper, 250 g button mushrooms, 2 onions, vegetables for salad*
TUES	Fish with tartar sauce*, chips, Ina's salad delight*	*Milk, 6-8 potatoes, 1 onion, pineapple*
WED	Lamb neck casserole*, carrots, green beans, rice	*2 onions, 4-6 carrots, green beans*
THURS	Sweet and tangy chicken*, savoury rice*, pumpkin, green beans, carrot salad (prepare Mum's curried peach salad* for Friday)	*Pumpkin, green beans, carrots, 2 oranges (if desired for carrot salad)*

FRI	Cold meats, frikkadels* (cold), sliced sweet melon, sliced pineapple, Mum's curried peach salad*, bread rolls	*Cold meats, sweet melon, pineapple, 2 onions, bread rolls*
SAT	Toast with cheese, ham and tomato	*Bread, cheese, tomato*
SUN	Braai (lamb chops, sausage), braai bread, mixed salad	*Cheese and tomato for braai bread, vegetables for salad*
MON	Agnes's noodles*, mixed salad	*1 onion, 1 green pepper, 1 tomato, 100 g Cheddar cheese, vegetables for salad*
TUES	Chicken Tetrazzini*, sliced tomatoes, creamstyle sweet-corn (Chicken Tetrazzini* doesn't appear later in the month; double nevertheless and use as needed)	*2 onions, 250 g button mushrooms, 375 ml milk, 150 g Cheddar cheese, 2 tomatoes*
WED	Eric's mock crayfish*, jacket potatoes, beetroot salad, sliced pineapple	*1 onion, 25 ml milk, 4-6 potatoes, beetroot (if preferred fresh), pineapple*
THURS	Aunt Minnie's tuna soufflé*, peas, squash, mixed salad	*1 onion, 100 g Cheddar cheese, 250 ml milk, 2-3 squash, vegetables for salad*
FRI	Hamburgers, chips	*Hamburger rolls, lettuce, onion, tomato, 6-8 potatoes*
SAT	Mavis's macaroni cheese*, mixed salad	*2 onions, 100 g Cheddar cheese, vegetables for salad*
SUN	All-time favourite beef*, rice, peas, carrots, beetroot salad	*250 g button mushrooms, 1 onion, 200 ml cream, 4-6 carrots, beetroot (if preferred fresh)*
MON	Fish cakes*, mashed potatoes, baby marrows with mushrooms, beans in tomato sauce	*2 onions, 4-6 potatoes, milk, 500 g baby marrows, 250 g button mushrooms*
TUES	Leftovers (clean out refrigerator)	

Desserts

Marshmallow fridge tart*	*4 bananas*
Ice cream with caramel sauce*	*250 ml milk*
Fruit salad	*Fruit*
Ice cream with chocolate sauce*	
Strawberry pudding*	
Jelly custard* with custard	*500 ml milk*

Shopping list

SPICES AND HERBS

- [ ] Black pepper
- [ ] Flavour enhancer
- [ ] Garlic powder
- [ ] Oregano
- [ ] Coarsely ground black pepper
- [ ] Thyme
- [ ] Garlic flakes
- [ ] Paprika
- [ ] Mixed herbs
- [ ] Turmeric
- [ ] Mild curry powder
- [ ] Basil
- [ ] Peri-peri

_____
_____
_____
_____

MEAT AND FISH

- [ ] 2 packets (4-6 pieces each) lamb chops
- [ ] 1,25 kg lamb neck chops
- [ ] 4-6 steaks
- [ ] 750 g tenderised steak
- [ ] 4-6 pork chops
- [ ] 1 x 750 g mince
- [ ] 2 x 500 g mince
- [ ] 1 kg mince
- [ ] 3 x sausage
- [ ] 4 x 800 g hake
- [ ] 3 packets (6-8 pieces each) chicken portions
- [ ] 4 packets (250 g each) rindless bacon
- [ ] 250 g garlic polony
- [ ] 350 g ham
- [ ] 500 g cold meats (own choice)
- [ ] 250 g Vienna sausages
- [ ] 1 packet hamburger patties

_____
_____
_____
_____
_____

GENERAL

- [ ] 750 g Cheddar cheese (omit if bought weekly – see fresh produce on menu)
- [ ] 200 g mozzarella cheese (omit if bought weekly – see fresh produce on menu)
- [ ] 1,5 kg margarine
- [ ] 2 litres ice cream (any flavour)
- [ ] 2 dozen eggs
- [ ] 1 bottle tomato sauce
- [ ] 1 bottle mayonnaise
- [ ] 2 bottles cooking oil
- [ ] 1 bottle chutney
- [ ] 1 bottle vinegar
- [ ] 1 small bottle lemon juice
- [ ] 1 small bottle Worcester sauce
- [ ] 1 small bottle Tabasco sauce
- [ ] 1 packet meat stock cubes
- [ ] 1 packet chicken stock cubes
- [ ] 2 packets cream of mushroom soup powder
- [ ] 1 packet oxtail soup powder
- [ ] 1 packet brown onion soup powder
- [ ] 2 kg rice
- [ ] 2,5 kg sugar
- [ ] 500 g macaroni
- [ ] 500 g spaghetti
- [ ] 500 g spinach noodles
- [ ] 2 packets (500 g each) shell noodles
- [ ] 1 kg cake flour
- [ ] 1 packet cornflour
- [ ] 500 g self-raising flour
- [ ] 1 small can baking powder
- [ ] 1 packet glacé cherries
- [ ] 1 packet Marie biscuits
- [ ] 1 packet (250 g) crispbread
- [ ] 1 can (410 g) evaporated milk
- [ ] 250 g seedless raisins
- [ ] 250 g dried apricots
- [ ] 1 packet crushed wheat or barley
- [ ] 7 cans (185 g each) tuna
- [ ] 1 can (425 g) pilchards in tomato sauce
- [ ] 2 cans (410 g each) tomato purée
- [ ] 2 cans (115 g each) tomato paste

- [ ] 1 can (425 g) tomato and onion mix
- [ ] 2 cans (410 g each) creamstyle sweetcorn
- [ ] 1 can (450 g) three-bean salad
- [ ] 2 bottles beetroot salad
- [ ] 3 cans (425 g each) beans in tomato sauce
- [ ] 5 cans (410 g each) peas or 1,75 kg frozen peas
- [ ] 1 can (425 g) pineapple pieces
- [ ] 1 can (825 g) sliced peaches in syrup
- [ ] 1 small can strawberry jam
- [ ] 1 small can apricot jam
- [ ] 1 packet marshmallows
- [ ] 1 packet strawberry jelly powder
- [ ] 2 packets jelly powder (any flavour)
- [ ] 1 small jar meat spread
- [ ] 1 small jar sandwich spread
- [ ] 125 ml sherry

Notes and birthdays

MENU	FRESH PRODUCE
MON Pasta à la Alana*	*1 onion, 3 tomatoes, 1 green pepper*
TUES Mince surprise*, mixed salad	*1 onion, vegetables for salad*
WED Grilled chicken drumsticks, Estelle's rice salad*, peas, carrot salad	*1 green pepper, 1 onion, 1 tomato, carrots, 2 oranges (if desired for carrot salad)*
THURS Frikkadels*, potatoes in onion sauce*, mixed salad, beans in tomato sauce	*2 slices white bread, 2 onions, 2 carrots, 8 potatoes, 100 ml milk, vegetables for salad*
FRI Pizza for Africa* (salami and mushrooms)	*200 g Cheddar cheese, 200 g mozzarella cheese, 250 g button mushrooms*
SAT Braaied lamb chops, roosterkoek*, sousboontjies, coleslaw*	*½ cabbage, 1 pineapple, 2 bananas, 25 ml milk*
SUN Chicken and asparagus tart*, hot rice salad*, beetroot salad, mixed salad	*250 ml milk, 1 small onion, 50 g Cheddar cheese, 1 large onion, 125 g button mushrooms, beetroot (if preferred fresh), vegetables for salad*
MON Elzan's bacon and noodles*, mixed salad	*1 onion, 50 g Cheddar cheese, vegetables for salad*
TUES Pork chops, yellow rice with raisins, glazed sweet potatoes*, green beans	*4-5 sweet potatoes, green beans, 1 onion, 1 potato*
WED Hamburgers, chips	*6-8 hamburger rolls, 1 tomato, 1 onion, lettuce, 6-8 large potatoes*
THURS Tuna noodle salad*, whole-wheat sandwiches	*1 large onion, 1 large tomato, 1 green pepper, 1 apple, lettuce, 8-12 slices whole-wheat bread*
FRI Braaied sausage, garlic rolls*, quick bean salad*, sliced tomatoes	*4-6 long rolls, 1 onion, 2 tomatoes*
SAT Wrapped frikkadels*, potatoes in onion sauce*, carrot salad, sliced pineapple	*6 potatoes, carrots for salad, 2 oranges (if desired for carrot salad), 1 pineapple*
SUN Rum and raisin chicken*, yellow rice, mixed salad	*1 lemon, vegetables for salad*
MON Rina's lasagne*, mixed salad	*2 onions, 1,25 litres milk, 100 g Cheddar cheese, vegetables for salad*
TUES Smoorsnoek dish*, tomato salad*	*3 onions, 1 lemon (optional), 3-4 tomatoes*

Day	Meal	Ingredients
WED	Chicken Tetrazzini*, mixed salad	2 onions, 250 g button mushrooms, vegetables for salad
THURS	Fish cakes*, mashed potatoes, peas, squash	1 onion, 6-8 potatoes, milk, 2-3 squash
FRI	Pizza for Africa* (bacon and mushrooms)	200 g Cheddar cheese, 200 g mozzarella cheese, 250 g button mushrooms
SAT	Braaied chicken (with King Arthur's chicken marinade*), sweet melon, Estelle's rice salad*, tomato salad*	4 onions, sweet melon, 1 green pepper, 4-5 tomatoes
SUN	Chicken Tetrazzini*, salami, sweet melon, carrot salad, sliced pineapple, watermelon	Sweet melon, carrots for salad, 2 oranges (if desired for carrot salad), 1 pineapple, watermelon
MON	Fish lasagne*, mixed salad	1 large onion, 500 ml milk, 100 g Cheddar cheese, vegetables for salad
TUES	Mince surprise*, carrot salad, mixed salad	1 onion, carrots, 2 oranges (if desired for carrot salad), vegetables for salad
WED	Braaied lamb chops, roosterkoek*, pineapple, sliced tomatoes, sousboontjies	1 pineapple, 2 tomatoes
THURS	Roast leg of lamb, pot-roast potatoes, creamy green beans*, glazed carrots, beetroot, baby marrow stir-fry*	4-6 potatoes, 2 onions, 2 tomatoes, 400 g baby marrows, 125 ml milk, 25 g Cheddar cheese, 5-7 carrots, beetroot (if preferred fresh)
FRI	Leftovers (clean out refrigerator)	
SAT	Hamburgers, chips	6-8 hamburger rolls, 6-8 large potatoes, 1 tomato, 1 onion, lettuce
SUN	Braaied steak, braaied bread (banana), three-bean salad*, carrot salad	4 ripe bananas, 8-12 slices bread, 1 onion, 1 green pepper, carrots, 2 oranges (if desired for carrot salad)
MON	Rina's lasagne*, mixed salad	Vegetables for salad
TUES	Eric's mock crayfish*	1 onion, 25 ml milk
WED	Fried sausage, rolls, sweet melon, watermelon	6-8 rolls, sweet melon, watermelon

Desserts

Dessert	Ingredients
Fruit salad, ice cream	Fruit for fruit salad
Trifle*	1 trifle sponge, 1,25 litres milk, 250 ml cream
Italian cream pudding*	750 ml milk
Banana jelly*, custard	2 bananas, 500 ml milk
Lemon custard tart*	600 ml milk, 250 ml cream
Ice cream, chocolate sauce*	
Chocolate sponge pudding*, ice cream	

Shopping list

SPICES AND HERBS

- [ ] Salt
- [ ] Black pepper
- [ ] Cayenne pepper
- [ ] Flavour enhancer
- [ ] Curry powder
- [ ] Parsley
- [ ] Garlic flakes
- [ ] Spice for rice
- [ ] Turmeric
- [ ] Ground ginger
- [ ] Cinnamon
- [ ] Garlic powder
- [ ] Nutmeg
- [ ] Paprika
- [ ] Oregano
- [ ] Basil

_____
_____
_____
_____

MEAT AND FISH

- [ ] 1 whole chicken
- [ ] 8-10 chicken drumsticks
- [ ] 2 chicken breasts (for chicken and asparagus tart)
- [ ] 6-8 chicken portions
- [ ] 4 x 500 g mince
- [ ] 2 x sausage
- [ ] 1 leg of lamb
- [ ] 2 packets (8-12 pieces each) lamb chops
- [ ] 4-6 steaks (own choice)
- [ ] 6-8 pork chops
- [ ] 450 g salami slices
- [ ] 1 whole salami
- [ ] 3 x 250 g diced bacon
- [ ] 12-16 hamburger patties
- [ ] 800 g hake

_____
_____
_____
_____

GENERAL

- [ ] 800 g Cheddar cheese (omit if bought weekly – see fresh produce on menu)
- [ ] 2 x 200 g mozzarella cheese (omit if bought fresh – see fresh produce on menu)
- [ ] 1,5 kg margarine
- [ ] 2 litres vanilla ice cream
- [ ] 3 dozen eggs
- [ ] 2 bottles chutney
- [ ] 1 bottle white vinegar
- [ ] 2 bottles cooking oil
- [ ] 1 bottle Worcester sauce
- [ ] 1 bottle Tabasco sauce
- [ ] 1 bottle tomato sauce
- [ ] 790 g mayonnaise
- [ ] 1 packet chicken marinade
- [ ] 2 packets mushroom sauce powder
- [ ] 1 packet oxtail soup powder
- [ ] 1 packet cream of mushroom soup powder
- [ ] 2 packets brown onion soup powder
- [ ] 2 cans (410 g each) minestrone
- [ ] 1 can (410 g) cream of chicken soup
- [ ] 1 can (410 g) tomato soup
- [ ] 3 kg rice
- [ ] 2 x 500 g shell noodles
- [ ] 500 g noodles (any kind)
- [ ] 875 g spinach noodles
- [ ] 1 kg self-raising flour
- [ ] 2 kg bread flour
- [ ] 1 kg cake flour
- [ ] 2 packets instant yeast
- [ ] 1 container custard powder
- [ ] 1 can cocoa
- [ ] 1 packet cream of tartar
- [ ] 1 small bottle rum essence
- [ ] 2,5 kg sugar
- [ ] 500 g seedless raisins
- [ ] 250 g sultanas
- [ ] 1 packet chopped walnuts (optional)
- [ ] 1 can (400 g) smoorsnoek
- [ ] 5 cans (200 g each) tuna
- [ ] 1 can (425 g) pilchards in tomato sauce

- [ ] 1 small can (225 g) mixed vegetables
- [ ] 2 cans (230 g each) sliced green beans
- [ ] 1 can (410 g) butter beans
- [ ] 5 cans (410 g each) tomato and onion mix
- [ ] 2 cans (115 g each) tomato paste
- [ ] 1 can (400 g) mushrooms
- [ ] 2 cans (410 g each) peas or 800 g frozen peas
- [ ] 3 cans (420 g each) beans in tomato sauce
- [ ] 1 can (410 g) asparagus
- [ ] 2 bottles sousboontjies
- [ ] 1 bottle beetroot (omit if bought fresh)
- [ ] 2 cans (410 g each) sliced peaches
- [ ] 1 can (410 g) fruit salad
- [ ] 1 can golden syrup
- [ ] 1 small bottle lemon juice
- [ ] 2 cans (397 g each) condensed milk
- [ ] 1 can (410 g) evaporated milk
- [ ] 1 packet red jelly powder
- [ ] 1 packet green jelly powder
- [ ] 1 packet lemon jelly powder
- [ ] 1 packet jelly powder (any kind)
- [ ] 1 packet Tennis biscuits
- [ ] 100 g Chick a Bix biscuits
- [ ] 1 roll heavy-duty tinfoil
- [ ] cocktail sticks
- [ ] 125 ml sweet wine

Notes and birthdays

Own menus for special occasions

BREAD AND ITS COMPANIONS

Bread remains popular, either as an accompaniment or as a light meal.

ROOSTERKOEK

(Knead the dough about 30 minutes before lighting the fire.)

1 kg bread flour
1 packet instant yeast
15 ml salt
600 ml lukewarm water
margarine

Combine the dry ingredients in a large mixing bowl. Add the water and mix. Grease your hands well with margarine and knead the dough for about 10-12 minutes. Use more margarine if needed. The dough must be firm enough to easily come loose from your hands, otherwise it is too slack and will not braai well over the coals. Cover with clingwrap and leave in a warm place for about 30-40 minutes.

Grease your hands with margarine again and knead the dough a few more times – not too much. Shape into balls and flatten them until they are about 3 cm thick. Place on a floured tray and sprinkle more flour lightly over the balls. This will prevent their sticking to the braai grid.

Braai for about 15 minutes over hot coals, or until cooked. Turn frequently. The rolls are ready if they sound hollow when tapped. It is, however, safer to break one open to make sure that they are cooked, as the cooking time can vary depending on the heat of the coals.

GARLIC ROLLS

4-6 long bread rolls
garlic spread*

Preheat the oven to 100°C (200°F). Slice each roll in 1,5 cm thick slices, without cutting right through. Spread the garlic spread liberally between the slices. Wrap each roll individually in tinfoil. Place the rolls in the oven for about 12 minutes. It should be just warm enough to melt the margarine.

If desired, the rolls can be heated in the tinfoil on the grid over the coals.

GARLIC BREAD

1 French loaf
150 g margarine
20 ml meat spread
10 ml garlic powder

Preheat the oven to 100°C (200°F). Slice the loaf into 1 cm thick slices, without cutting right through. Mix the margarine, meat spread and garlic powder. Spread the mixture liberally between the slices and wrap the loaf in tinfoil. Place in the oven for 20 minutes. Serve hot.

GARLIC SPREAD

125 g soft margarine

5 ml garlic powder

10 ml dried parsley

5 ml flavour enhancer

Mix the ingredients well and store in a dish with a tight-fitting lid in the refrigerator. It's also delicious on boiled potatoes.

QUICK CHEESE SNACKS

1 tub (250 g) smooth cottage cheese

8-10 slices rye bread

4-5 slices salami, ham or tomato, shredded

5 ml black pepper

325 ml grated Cheddar cheese

Spread the cottage cheese on the slices of bread. Sprinkle shredded salami, ham or tomato over and sprinkle with pepper. Sprinkle the Cheddar cheese over and grill in the oven until the cheese has melted. Serve with coleslaw* or a mixed salad.

CHEESE SAUCE SURPRISE

250 g bacon, shredded

6-8 slices toast or rolls (halved)

375 ml grated Cheddar cheese

500 ml basic white sauce*

cayenne pepper to taste

Preheat the oven to 210°C (400°F).

   Fry the bacon lightly in a pan. Arrange the toast or rolls on a greased baking sheet. Spoon the bacon on top. Stir the cheese into the hot white sauce and add the pepper. Stir well and spoon the sauce on top of the toast or rolls. Place in the oven and bake until the cheese sauce starts to brown.

More hints for interesting sandwich fillings

- *Peanut butter and golden syrup are delicious on a sandwich, but why not add a few slices of banana?*
- *Ever tried beetroot and cheese together?*
- *Another unusual combination that tastes marvellous: lettuce, cheese and a thin layer of apricot jam.*
- *Chicken and mayonnaise with a thin slice of pineapple, or grated pineapple, is food fit for a king.*
- *Pineapple, ham and a touch of mustard sauce make a tasty combination.*
- *A lettuce leaf for colour, sandwich spread for flavour, and ham make a delicious combination.*
- *Combine finely chopped hard-boiled eggs with grated cheese and chopped parsley.*
- *Grated cheese and raisins make a delicious, and healthy, filling. Add a little salad dressing to the cheese, if you wish.*
- *Grated apple and tuna are also an unusually tasty combination.*
- *Chutney and cheese – simple but delicious!*

CHEESE AND HERB LOAF

500 g self-raising flour

5 ml dried oregano

75 ml dried parsley

5 ml salt

5 ml garlic flakes

pinch of cayenne pepper

500 ml buttermilk

1 egg

grated Cheddar cheese and paprika for sprinkling

Preheat the oven to 180°C (350°F). Grease a 23 x 8 x 8 cm loaf pan and sprinkle lightly with flour.

Mix the dry ingredients. Beat the buttermilk and egg together. Stir into the dry ingredients and mix well to make a dough. Spoon the dough into the loaf pan and smooth the top. Sprinkle cheese and paprika over and bake for 1 hour.

VERSATILE TUNA FILLING

1 can (200 g) tuna, drained

1 onion, chopped

1 tomato, chopped

125 ml grated Cheddar cheese

salt and pepper

25 ml mayonnaise

Mix all the ingredients together well. This mixture is delicious on toasted sandwiches or as a filling for baked potatoes.

PIZZA FOR AFRICA

CRUST

4 x 250 ml self-raising flour

300 ml boiling water

250 ml cooking oil

pinch of salt

FILLING

2 cans (410 g each) tomato and onion mix

500 ml grated Cheddar cheese

200 g ham, shredded

250 ml canned pineapple pieces, drained

200 g mozzarella cheese, grated

2 ml dried oregano

Preheat the oven to 180°C (350°F).

Place all the crust ingredients in a container with a tight-fitting lid. Shake the container well until a dough forms. Gently the dough into two 35 x 25 x 2 cm swiss roll pans.

Spread the tomato and onion mix over the dough. Sprinkle the Cheddar cheese over evenly. Arrange the ham and pineapple pieces on top of the cheese. Sprinkle the mozzarella cheese over and then the oregano.
Bake for 15-20 minutes on the middle rack of the oven until the cheese starts to brown.

VARIATIONS

Instead of ham and pineapple pieces, use one of the following combinations:

200 g salami, shredded and

16 button mushrooms, shredded

or

200 g bacon, shredded and

16 button mushrooms, shredded

RIGHT: Cheese and Herb Loaf

DELICIOUS SOUPS

Soup is filling, nutritious and economical. It makes a complete meal with bread, and is marvellous for entertaining at the fireside on a cold winter's night.

ALL-IN-ONE SOUP##

¾ packet (375 g) split peas
water
4 large carrots, peeled and coarsely grated
2 potatoes, peeled and grated
2 tomatoes, peeled and chopped
3 onions, chopped
150 g broccoli, broken into florets
37,5 ml Worcester sauce
37,5 ml tomato sauce
10 ml sugar
10 ml celery salt
5 ml garlic flakes
salt and pepper to taste
2 handfuls pasta
125 g bacon, shredded and fried

Rinse the peas thoroughly and place in a pressure cooker. Fill the cooker to two-thirds full with water and pressure-cook for 15 minutes. Add the rest of the ingredients, except the pasta and bacon. Pressure-cook for a further 20 minutes. Add more water if the soup is too thick. Allow to simmer for an hour without the pressure gauge. Add the pasta and bacon and simmer until the pasta is soft.

PEA SOUP

375 g split peas
2 litres cold water
1 onion, grated
1 carrot, peeled and finely grated
1 beef stock cube
250 ml boiling water
3 ml mixed spice
5 ml paprika
5 ml celery salt
2 ml black pepper
salt to taste
500 ml shredded cooked pork sausage

Rinse the peas well in cold water. Place the peas in a pressure cooker with the 2 litres of cold water. Add the grated onion, carrot and stock cube. Cover with the lid and pressure-cook for 25 minutes. Add the rest of the ingredients, except the pork sausage, and replace the lid, without the pressure gauge. Cook for a further 30 minutes. Add the pork sausage and cook for a further 15 minutes.

> ## Tip
> *If you have a glut of tomatoes, slice the tomatoes and dry them in the sun. Store in bottles and use in soup and other dishes when they are scarce and expensive.*

CATHI HEMPEL'S CURRIED BUTTERNUT SOUP

1,5 kg butternut squash, peeled and cubed

1 medium onion, chopped

5 ml mild curry powder

5 ml garlic flakes

5 ml mixed herbs

black pepper to taste

250 ml pure orange juice

500 ml chicken stock

cream or sour cream and dried parsley (optional)

Cook the butternut and onion in a little water until soft. Add the curry powder, garlic flakes, mixed herbs and black pepper and stir well. Mix half the orange juice and chicken stock with half the butternut mixture. Mix until smooth with a mixer or beater and repeat with the remaining half. The soup can be thinned to taste with orange juice or chicken stock. Serve hot. If desired, stir a little cream or sour cream and parsley gently into the soup.

FARM SOUP

250 g brown sugar beans, soaked overnight in water

3,25 litres water

250 g rindless shoulder bacon, shredded

2 cloves garlic, crushed

2 stalks celery, cut into rings

12,5 ml margarine

4 carrots, peeled and grated

3 medium potatoes, peeled and grated

2 onions, chopped

250 g cauliflower, cut into florets

25 ml Worcester sauce

5 ml flavour enhancer

7 ml coarsely ground black pepper

1 can (65 g) tomato paste

Drain the beans and add 750 ml of the water. Cook the beans in the water until soft. Meanwhile, fry the bacon, garlic and celery in the margarine over moderate heat for 5-6 minutes. Add all the remaining ingredients to the beans and add the remaining 2,5 litres of water. Cook for 2-3 hours or until the vegetables are soft. Serve hot with fresh bread or rolls.

> ### Tip
> *If soup is too salty, add a few slices of raw potato to get rid of the saltiness.*

MUM 'S BEAN SOUP

500 g sugar beans, soaked overnight in water

2,5 litres water

250 g rindless bacon, shredded

1 large onion, cut into rings

500 g lamb shank

5 ml black pepper

pinch of salt

Drain the beans and place in a saucepan with the water. Heat to boiling point and add all the other ingredients. Reduce the heat and allow to simmer for about 2 hours or until the beans are soft. Serve hot with fresh bread.

> ### Tip
> *If there's a fatty layer on top of soup, add a few ice cubes; the fat will cling to the ice.*

SPLENDID SALADS

A selection of delectable salads, some of which can also be served as a light meal. All are quick and easy to make, and just a little different from the usual.

ESTELLE'S RICE SALAD

500 ml cold cooked rice

1 green pepper, shredded

1 onion, shredded

1 tomato, shredded

125 ml canned peaches, shredded

125 ml seedless raisins

30 ml chutney

5 ml curry powder

125 ml mayonnaise

Mix the rice, green pepper, onion, tomato, peaches and raisins in a salad bowl. Combine the rest of the ingredients and stir lightly into the salad.

RICE SALAD

3 bananas, peeled and sliced

15 ml lemon juice

500 ml cold cooked rice

100 ml chopped green pepper

150 ml shredded pineapple

1 large tomato, chopped

75 ml mayonnaise

15 ml tomato sauce

5 ml flavour enhancer

5 ml paprika

fresh parsley for garnishing (optional)

Sprinkle the bananas with the lemon juice. Mix the bananas, rice, green pepper, pineapple and tomato. Combine the mayonnaise, tomato sauce, flavour enhancer and paprika and pour over the rice mixture. Mix lightly. Garnish with fresh parsley, if desired.

COLESLAW

½ cabbage

125 ml sultanas

1 pineapple, peeled and grated

2 bananas, peeled and shredded

125 ml mayonnaise

25 ml condensed milk

25 ml fresh milk

Soak the cabbage in salted water to remove bugs and other undesirables. Drain and grate finely. Add the sultanas, pineapple and bananas. Mix the mayonnaise, condensed milk and fresh milk and add to the cabbage mixture. Mix lightly.

Tip

Dip bananas or avocado pears, peel and all, in boiling water for 2 seconds to prevent discoloration.

RIGHT: Estelle's Rice Salad

HOT RICE SALAD

1 large onion, chopped
12,5 ml cooking oil
65 g bacon, shredded
125 g button mushrooms, shredded
500 ml cooked rice
5 ml garlic flakes
5 ml spice for rice

Fry the chopped onion in the oil until lightly browned. Add the bacon and mushrooms and sauté until cooked. Add the cooked rice, garlic flakes and spice and heat until very hot. Serve the salad hot.

TROPICAL POTATO SALAD

5 large, unpeeled potatoes, cooked in water with a pinch of salt
100 ml crushed pineapple
75 ml mayonnaise
15 ml condensed milk

Allow potatoes to cool. Peel off the skins and cube the potatoes. Place in a salad bowl. Mix the rest of the ingredients and spoon over the potato cubes. Mix lightly.

TUNA SALAD

2 cans (185 g each) tuna, drained
100 ml pineapple chunks
150 ml cooked peas
1 large tomato, chopped
lettuce, chopped (optional)
5 ml flavour enhancer
3 ml black pepper
45 ml mayonnaise
5 ml tomato sauce

Flake the tuna and mix it with the pineapple, peas, tomato and lettuce. Mix the spices, mayonnaise and tomato sauce and stir into the tuna mixture.

TUNA NOODLE SALAD

250 ml shell noodles, cooked and cooled
2 cans (200 g each) tuna, drained and flaked
1 large tomato, chopped
1 onion, chopped
1 green pepper, chopped
1 apple, chopped
200 ml mayonnaise
pinch of salt
3 ml curry powder
12,5 ml chutney
4-6 lettuce leaves

Mix the noodles, tuna, tomato, onion, green pepper and apple in a salad bowl. Mix the rest of the ingredients, except the lettuce leaves, and pour over the tuna mixture. Stir lightly to mix. Serve on the lettuce leaves.

QUICK BEAN SALAD

1 can (420 g) beans in tomato sauce
1 onion, chopped
25 ml mayonnaise

Mix all the ingredients in a salad bowl.

Tip

Add a tablespoonful of cooking oil to the water in which beetroot is cooked to prevent it boiling over.

THREE-BEAN SALAD

1 can (420 g) beans in tomato sauce

1 can (410 g) butter beans, drained

1 can (230 g) sliced green beans, drained

1 onion, chopped

1 green pepper, chopped

25 ml cooking oil

150 ml white vinegar

100 ml sugar

5 ml basil

Mix the beans, onion and green pepper in a salad bowl. Mix the rest of the ingredients and add to the beans. Stir well.

This salad is even better if it is allowed to stand for a day or two.

The salad can also be bottled and stored in the refrigerator for quite a few weeks.

BANANA AND BEAN SALAD

1 can (425 g) beans in tomato sauce

30 ml mayonnaise

15 ml tomato sauce

3 ml black pepper

3 ml flavour enhancer

3 bananas, peeled and sliced

5 ml lemon juice

3 ml paprika

Place the beans in tomato sauce in a salad bowl and stir in the mayonnaise and tomato sauce.

Sprinkle the spices over. Sprinkle the bananas with lemon juice and stir into the bean mixture. Sprinkle with paprika. Refrigerate the salad until just before serving.

> ## Tip
> *Add a tablespoonful of vinegar to the water in which beetroot is cooked to cook it quicker.*

RINA'S POPULAR BANANA SALAD

5 ripe, firm bananas

5 dried apricots, shredded

125 ml granadilla yoghurt

37,5 ml condensed milk

Slice the bananas into a salad bowl. Add the shredded apricots. Mix the yoghurt and condensed milk and add to the fruit. Mix lightly with a fork.

INA'S SALAD DELIGHT

1 can (450 g) three-bean salad

500 ml cold cooked crushed wheat or barley

1 onion, chopped

200 ml chopped pineapple

150 ml seedless raisins

DRESSING

40 ml oil

80 ml water

3 ml black pepper

5 ml flavour enhancer

3 ml oregano

Mix all the salad ingredients together in a salad bowl.

Place all the dressing ingredients in a bottle with a cork and shake well. Pour the dressing over the and mix lightly. Refrigerate the salad for at least 24 hours before serving.

MUM'S CURRIED PEACH SALAD

2 onions, grated

15 ml oil

8 ml mild curry powder

150 ml white vinegar

3 ml turmeric

200 ml sugar

3 ml salt

5 ml cornflour

1 can (825 g) sliced peaches in syrup

75 ml seedless raisins

Sauté the onions in the oil until soft but not brown. Mix the curry powder with 30 ml vinegar and add to the onions.

Mix the turmeric, sugar, salt and cornflour with the remaining vinegar and the syrup from the peaches. Add the cornflour mixture to the onions and stir well. Add the raisins and simmer over low heat for 15 minutes. Stir often.

Halve the peach slices and add to the curry sauce. Simmer for 10 minutes. Cool and refrigerate. This salad will keep for quite a few days in the refrigerator.

TOMATO SALAD

3-4 tomatoes

2 onions, chopped

100 ml water

5 ml lemon juice

30 ml chutney

5 ml salt

5 ml black pepper

Cut the tomatoes into 6 mm thick slices and quarter the slices. Add the onions. Mix the rest of the ingredients and pour over the tomatoes.

Tip

To freshen lettuce, place it in ice cold water with a little sugar added and refrigerate for about 30 minutes.

RAW VEGETABLE SALAD

250 ml carrots, cut into strips

250 ml button mushrooms, sliced

250 ml cauliflower, chopped

250 ml tomatoes, cubed

250 ml baby marrows, cut into rings

125 ml green peppers, cut into julienne strips

DRESSING

45 ml cooking oil

30 ml lemon juice

100 ml water

3 ml coarsely ground black pepper

3 ml mixed herbs

Mix all the salad ingredients and refrigerate.

Place the dressing ingredients in a bottle with a cork and shake very well. Pour the required quantity over the salad.

Tip

A lemon and a little salt will keep the bread board beautifully clean and white.

TEMPTING VEGETABLES

Vegetables are essential in a healthy diet, and these dishes will make even reluctant eaters' mouths water.

POTATOES IN ONION SAUCE

6 large potatoes, unpeeled and scrubbed
125 ml margarine
1 packet brown onion soup powder
5 ml dried parsley

Preheat the oven to 160°C (325°F).

Cut the potatoes in 1 cm slices, without cutting right through; the potatoes must remain whole at the base. Pack the potatoes alongside one another in an ovenproof dish with a lid.

Melt the margarine and stir in the onion soup powder and parsley. Pour the soup mixture over the potatoes and cover. Bake for about 2 hours in the oven until the potatoes are soft. If the potatoes get too dry, add a little boiling water. Serve hot.

MICROWAVE METHOD

Follow the recipe to the point where the soup mixture is poured over the potatoes. Cover and microwave for 14-16 minutes on 100% power. Allow to stand for 5 minutes before removing the lid.

> ### Tip
> *Pour boiling water over raw potato chips. Dry and fry as usual. The chips will be delightfully crisp.*

POTATO BAKE

6 potatoes
250 ml fresh cream
1 packet brown onion soup powder

Peel the potatoes and cut into 7 mm thick slices. Pack the slices in a greased ovenproof dish and cover with a layer of cream and a layer of onion soup powder. Repeat the layers until all the ingredients have been used. Bake for 1-1¼ hours at 180°C (350°F) or until the potatoes are soft.

GLAZED SWEET POTATOES

200 ml sugar
25 ml butter
1 ml ground ginger
2 ml ground cinnamon or 2-3 pieces stick cinnamon
12,5 ml golden syrup
4-5 medium sweet potatoes, peeled and sliced
pinch of salt
50 ml water

Place the sugar, butter, ginger, cinnamon and syrup in a saucepan and cook over low heat until starting to brown. Add the sweet potatoes, salt and water. Cook over moderate heat until the sweet potatoes are soft and the sauce is sticky.

ORANGE SWEET POTATOES

4-5 fairly large sweet potatoes, peeled and sliced

125 ml water

pinch of salt

12,5 ml butter

125 ml sugar

12,5 ml golden syrup

juice of 1 orange

5 ml grated orange peel

Boil the sweet potatoes in the water with a pinch of salt until soft. Add the rest of the ingredients and cook over low heat for a further 15 minutes. Stir lightly before serving.

SWEET PUMPKIN

2 slices onion

25 ml butter

750 g peeled ripe "boer" pumpkin or butternut squash, sliced

150 ml brown sugar

2 ml ground cinnamon

pinch of salt

pinch of black pepper

25 ml water

Fry the onion lightly in the butter until transparent. Add the pumpkin and then the rest of the ingredients. Do not stir. Cover and cook over low heat until the pumpkin is soft. Remove the lid and fry the pumpkin until the sauce is sticky. Stir lightly.

Tip

Add vinegar to the water in which cabbage is cooked, or place a slice of bread on top, to absorb the cooking odours.

Tip

Rub a little sugar into your palms to remove onion odours. Remember, too, to wash your hands in cold water after working with onions.

GRANDMA STELLA'S PUMPKIN FRITTERS

500 g "boer" pumpkin, cooked until tender in water and drained well

1 egg

60 ml self-raising flour

2 ml salt

125 ml cooking oil

45 ml sugar

10 ml ground cinnamon

Mash the pumpkin and stir in the egg, self-raising flour and salt. Heat the oil in a pan over moderate heat and spoon in tablespoonfuls of pumpkin. Fry on both sides until lightly browned. Sprinkle with a mixture of sugar and cinnamon and serve hot.

MARSHMALLOW SQUASH

3-4 squash, halved

500 ml water

3 ml salt

6-8 marshmallows

10 ml sugar

5 ml ground cinnamon

Boil the squash in the salted water for 20 minutes or until soft. Remove the squash from the water and discard the seeds. Place a marshmallow in each squash and sprinkle a mixture of sugar and cinnamon over each marshmallow.

Place the squash in an ovenproof dish and grill for 5-10 minutes in the oven or until the marshmallows have melted and browned slightly.

RIGHT: Glazed sweet potatoes

CREAMY SQUASH

2-3 large squash, halved and seeded

1 ml garlic powder (or to taste)

5 ml dried parsley

salt and pepper to taste

15 ml coffee creamer or 25 ml fresh cream

Boil the squash in water until soft and spoon the flesh from the shells. Drain very well. Mash well. Add the rest of the ingredients and mix well.

CARROTS IN ORANGE SAUCE

5 fairly large carrots, peeled and cubed

pinch of salt

100 ml orange juice

5 ml grated orange peel

75 ml sugar

12,5 ml custard powder

Boil the carrots in a little salted water until soft. Drain. Mix the rest of the ingredients and add to the carrots. Simmer slowly until the sauce thickens.

MICROWAVE METHOD

Place the carrots and a pinch of salt in a glass dish with a lid. Add 12,5 ml water. Cover with the lid and microwave for 10 minutes on 100% power. Mix the rest of the ingredients and pour over the carrots. Cover with the lid and microwave for a further 3 minutes on 70% power.

JUST CARROTS

400 g carrots, peeled and cut into rings

2 small potatoes, peeled and cubed

3 ml flavour enhancer

5 ml salt

350 ml water

Place all the ingredients in a saucepan and boil for about 45 minutes or until the carrots are soft. (Add a little water if the carrots boil dry and are still hard.) Serve hot.

BABY MARROWS WITH MUSHROOMS

250 g button mushrooms, rinsed and sliced

500 g baby marrows, cut into rings

1 large onion, cut into rings

50 g butter or margarine

3 ml black pepper

3 ml flavour enhancer

10 ml tomato purée

5 ml sugar

Fry the mushrooms, baby marrows and onion for 5 minutes in butter or margarine, or until the onion is translucent. Add the rest of the ingredients and stir well. Cover and simmer for 20 minutes. Remove the lid and simmer for a further 5 minutes. Serve hot with any meat dish or as a hot salad.

Tip

Add a tin (410 g) creamstyle sweetcorn and 250 ml cream to the Baby Marrows with Mushroom. Liquidise it for a wonderfully creamy soup.

BABY MARROW STIR-FRY

1 large onion, chopped
25 ml oil
1 large ripe tomato, skinned and sliced
400 g baby marrows, cut into rings
salt and black pepper to taste
5 ml sugar

Sauté the chopped onion lightly in the oil. Add the rest of the ingredients and stir-fry over moderate heat until cooked.

CREAMY GREEN BEANS

125 ml shredded bacon
1 onion, chopped
1 tomato, skinned and chopped
1 can (410 g) green beans, drained
salt and pepper
125 ml basic white sauce*
60 ml grated Cheddar cheese

Fry the bacon and onion until cooked. Add the tomato and stir-fry for a while. Add the beans and salt and pepper and bring the mixture to the boil again.
   Meanwhile, make the white sauce and stir in the cheese. Stir the cheese sauce into the bean mixture. Serve hot.

BACON BEANS

500 g fresh green beans
250 g rindless bacon
30 ml butter or margarine
15 ml oil
5 ml coarsely ground black pepper

Top and tail the beans and divide them into bundles of 5-6 beans each. Tie each bundle with a bacon rasher and secure with a cocktail stick. Melt the butter or margarine and oil in a pan and fry the bacon beans over moderate heat.

Sprinkle pepper over while frying. Turn often and remove from the stove when the bacon is cooked. Serve hot.

SPICY RICE

300 ml uncooked rice
5 ml margarine
5 ml spice for rice
2 ml paprika

Boil the rice in the usual way, adding the remaining ingredients instead of salt.

SAVOURY RICE

90 g margarine
250 ml uncooked rice
750 ml boiling water
5 ml flavour enhancer
30 ml tomato sauce
10 ml fruit chutney
5 ml dried parsley
3 ml mixed herbs

Melt the margarine in a saucepan and add the rice. Fry the rice over moderate heat until at least 75% of the rice has puffed up. Add the boiling water and stir in the rest of the ingredients. Cover with the lid and boil the rice for 15 minutes. Remove the lid and boil until the rice is dry. Serve hot.

> *Tip*
>
> *Add a few slices of onion to the potato chips in hot oil; it gives a marvellous flavour.*

LIGHT AND FILLING

These dishes are quick and easy to prepare if you get unexpected visitors. They're also really tasty and will always earn you compliments. Some are suitable for vegetarians.

PASTA À LA ALANA

250 g shell noodles
1 onion, chopped
3 tomatoes, chopped
1 whole salami, grated
6 hard-boiled eggs, chopped
1 green pepper, chopped
salt, pepper and flavour enhancer to taste
25 ml chutney
mayonnaise to taste

Boil the noodles according to the instructions on the packet. Drain and cool completely.

Mix all the ingredients together and allow to stand for a little while to let the flavours mingle.

PASTA À LA ALRINA

1 packet (500 g) small shell noodles
1 large onion, chopped
250 g button mushrooms, sliced
250 g rindless shoulder bacon, shredded
30 ml oil
1 packet cream of mushroom soup powder
400 ml water
5 ml coarsely ground black pepper
5 ml oregano

Boil the noodles until soft according to the instructions on the packet and drain.

Preheat the oven to 180°C (350°F).

Meanwhile, fry the onion, mushrooms and bacon in the oil until the onion is soft. Mix the soup with the water and boil until thick. Add the black pepper and oregano. Layer the noodles, bacon mixture and soup into a greased oven-proof dish and bake for 30 minutes.

AGNES'S NOODLES

250 g small shell noodles
1 large onion, chopped
1 small green pepper, chopped
50 g margarine or butter
2 cans (185 g each) tuna, drained
1 large tomato, skinned and grated
3 ml flavour enhancer
5 ml oregano
3 ml coarsely ground black pepper
3 ml basil
250 ml grated Cheddar cheese

Boil the noodles according to the instructions on the packet and drain.

Preheat the oven to 180°C (350°F).

Fry the onion and green pepper in the margarine or butter until the onion is translucent. Add the tuna. Add the remaining ingredients, except the cheese, and stir well. Simmer slowly until most of the water has evaporated. Layer the noodles and tuna in a greased ovenproof dish. Sprinkle the cheese over and bake for 15 minutes. Serve hot with a mixed salad.

> ### Tip
> *Why not prepare a pasta dish as individual portions? It always looks very impressive.*

ELZAN'S BACON AND NOODLES

500 g noodles (any kind)

cooking oil

250 g bacon, shredded

1 onion, chopped

1 can (410 g) cream of chicken soup

125 ml grated Cheddar cheese

1 can (400 g) mushrooms, drained

Boil the noodles according to the instructions on the packet. Drain and stir in a little cooking oil.

Meanwhile, fry the bacon and onion. Add the soup, cheese and mushrooms and stir until the mixture is very hot and the cheese has melted.

Spoon this mixture over the noodles and stir lightly. Serve hot.

MACARONI CHEESE

200 g (375 ml) macaroni

5 ml margarine

2 ripe tomatoes

salt and pepper

150 g (375 ml) grated Cheddar cheese

2 eggs

500 ml milk

a few pats butter or margarine for dotting

Boil the macaroni pieces according to the packet instructions, in boiling salted water to which the margarine has been added. Drain the macaroni when soft and place in a fairly large, greased ovenproof dish.

Preheat the oven to 180°C (350°F).

Meanwhile, cover the tomatoes with boiling water. Leave for a minute or two, then peel off the skins. Slice the tomatoes and arrange them on top of the cooked macaroni. Season with salt and pepper to taste. Sprinkle the cheese over.

Beat the eggs and milk together and add a little salt and pepper. Pour the egg and milk mixture over the macaroni in the dish. Dot with a few pats of butter or margarine. Bake for about 40 minutes or until set.

MAVIS'S MACARONI CHEESE

500 g macaroni

250 g rindless bacon, chopped

2 onions, finely chopped

15 ml butter or margarine

15 ml oil

3 eggs

125 ml tomato purée

3 ml flavour enhancer

3 ml garlic salt

250 ml grated Cheddar cheese

3 ml dried parsley

Boil the macaroni until soft, according to the instructions on the packet. Drain.

Preheat the oven to 180°C (350°F).

Meanwhile, fry the bacon and onions in a mixture of the butter or margarine and oil until the onions are lightly browned. Add the onions and bacon to the macaroni and stir.

Beat the eggs and add the tomato purée, flavour enhancer and garlic salt. Stir well and add to the macaroni mixture. Mix well and spoon into a greased ovenproof dish. Sprinkle the cheese and parsley over. Bake for about 30 minutes or until the cheese browns. Serve with a mixed salad.

QUICK SAVOURY TART

500 ml basic white sauce*

250 ml Vienna sausages, sliced

250 ml rindless bacon, shredded

250 ml grated Cheddar cheese

1 can (300 g) corned beef, shredded

4 eggs, beaten

10 ml dried parsley

Preheat the oven to 180°C (350°F).

Mix all the ingredients except the parsley and spoon into a large greased pie dish. Sprinkle the parsley over and bake for 40 minutes.

AUNT MARIE'S TUNA TART

1 thick slice white bread, broken into small pieces

250 ml milk

60 g butter or margarine

3 eggs, beaten

1 onion, grated

5 ml baking powder

2 cans (185 g each) tuna, drained

5 ml dried parsley

Preheat the oven to 180°C (350°F).

Place the bread, milk and butter or margarine in a saucepan and heat to boiling point. Combine the remaining ingredients. Remove the milk mixture from the stove and add the rest of the ingredients. Mix well and spoon into a greased pie dish. Bake for 25 minutes or until the tart begins to brown. Serve hot with a mixed salad.

CHICKEN AND ASPARAGUS TART

CRUST

100 g Chick a Bix biscuits, crushed

20 ml margarine, melted

FILLING

2 eggs, separated

250 ml basic white sauce*

250 ml cooked chicken, finely chopped

1 can (410 g) asparagus, drained

10 ml dried parsley

1 small onion, chopped

salt and pepper to taste

1 ml cayenne pepper

grated Cheddar cheese for sprinkling

Preheat the oven to 180°C (350°F).

Prepare the crust: Mix the crumbs with the margarine and press into a 20 x 20 x 5 cm pie dish. Bake for 10 minutes.

Prepare the filling: Stir the beaten egg yolks

into the white sauce. Add the chicken and asparagus. Stir in the other ingredients, except the egg whites and cheese. Fold in the stiffly whisked egg whites and spoon the mixture into the crust. Sprinkle the cheese over.
Bake for about 20 minutes, until the filling browns on top.

MICROWAVE METHOD

Crust: Use a round or oval dish and microwave for 2 minutes on 100% power.
Tart: Microwave for 8 minutes on 100% power.

Tip

Add 1-2 tablespoonfuls fresh breadcrumbs to the eggs when making scrambled eggs. This increases the quantity and adds a pleasant flavour.

BASIC WHITE SAUCE

30 ml margarine

30 ml cake flour

pinch of salt

250 ml milk

Melt the margarine in a saucepan over low heat. Add the flour and salt and stir well with a wooden spoon. Add the milk a little at a time, and stir constantly until the sauce thickens.

MICROWAVE METHOD

Microwave all the ingredients in a deep 750 ml dish on 100% power for 3 minutes. Stir well after each minute to prevent lumps forming.

LEFT: Quick savoury tart

CHICKEN TETRAZZINI

500 g shell noodles

2 onions, finely chopped

250 g button mushrooms, shredded

65 g bacon, shredded

30 ml cooking oil

1 packet cream of mushroom soup powder

1 can (410 g) evaporated milk

375 ml milk

1 cooked chicken, boned and finely chopped

375 ml grated Cheddar cheese

Boil the noodles in salted water until soft and drain.

Preheat the oven to 180°C (350°F). Meanwhile, fry the onions, mushrooms and bacon lightly in oil until cooked. Mix the soup powder, evaporated milk and fresh milk and add to the onion mixture. Stir constantly over low heat until the mixture thickens. Add the chicken and stir well.

Grease two ovenproof dishes. Divide the mixture in two and spoon into the dishes. Sprinkle the cheese over and bake for 15-20 minutes until the cheese browns.

Freeze one dish for later use.

Tip

The second dish can also be frozen unbaked. Thaw for a while before use and bake for 25 minutes in the oven preheated to 180°C (350°F).

CHEESY POTATOES

4-6 large potatoes

500 ml basic white sauce*

250 ml grated Cheddar cheese

cayenne pepper and salt to taste

1 ml paprika

Boil the unpeeled potatoes in salted water until soft.

Meanwhile, make the white sauce and stir in the rest of the ingredients. Stir well.

Quarter the potatoes (flat sides), but do not cut right through. Pull the quarters slightly apart and pour the hot sauce over. Serve hot.

POTATO AND ONION DELIGHT

6 potatoes, peeled and cubed

3 onions, chopped

2 large ripe tomatoes, skinned and cubed

250 g button mushrooms, rinsed and sliced

250 g bacon, shredded

1 apple, peeled and cubed

salt and pepper

15 ml margarine

Preheat the oven to 180°C (350°F).

Mix all the ingredients, except the margarine, and spoon into a fairly large greased ovenproof dish with a lid. Dot the mixture with margarine. Bake for 1 hour.

VARIATION

This dish is also delicious as a braai accompaniment. Place all the ingredients on a large sheet of tinfoil and dot with margarine. Close the tinfoil securely and place to one side over the coals until cooked.

RIGHT: Potato and onion delight

BASIC PANCAKES

250 ml water
125 ml milk
2 eggs
250 ml cake flour
5 ml baking powder
pinch of salt
12,5 ml brandy or vinegar
125 ml cooking oil

Beat the water, milk and eggs together. Gradually beat in the flour and baking powder and continue beating until the mixture is smooth. Add the salt and brandy or vinegar and beat well.

Preheat a suitable pan to very hot on top of the stove. Add just enough oil to grease the pan. Using a soup ladle, drop spoonfuls of batter (according to the size of the pan) into the pan. The batter should not form a thick layer in the pan. As soon as the edges of the pancake begin to recede from the sides of the pan, turn the pancake over. Bake for about 30 seconds on the other side and turn out onto a plate.

Keep a cup with a little oil to one side. Add half a teaspoon of oil to the pan after every second or third pancake. The recipe makes about 8 pancakes.

MINCE PANCAKES

2 x basic pancake recipe*
1 onion, chopped
12,5 ml cooking oil
500 g mince
25 ml chutney
25 ml tomato sauce
1 packet cream of mushroom soup powder
125 ml water
pepper

CHEESE SAUCE

500 ml basic white sauce*
250 ml grated Cheddar cheese
paprika
cayenne pepper

Make the pancakes as described.

Fry the chopped onion in the oil until browned. Add the mince and fry until cooked. Stir from time to time. Mix the chutney, tomato sauce, soup powder, water and pepper and add to the meat. Simmer for 10 minutes.

Preheat the oven to 180°C (350°F).

Spoon mince in the centre of each pancake and close it up like an envelope. Pack the pancakes tightly together in an ovenproof dish.

Prepare the white sauce and add the cheese, paprika and cayenne pepper. Mix well and pour over the pancakes. Bake for about 20 minutes, or until the cheese sauce starts to brown.

SWEET PANCAKES

3 x basic pancake recipe* (for a light meal) or 2 x basic pancake recipe* (for a dessert)
cinnamon sugar

Make the pancakes as described in the recipe and sprinkle over cinnamon sugar to taste.

QUICK FISH DISHES

These economical fish dishes can be made all year round, as fresh or frozen hake and canned fish are used to make them.

AUNT MINNIE'S TUNA SOUFFLÉ

2 cans (185 g each) tuna, drained and flaked
1 large onion, finely chopped
250 ml grated Cheddar cheese
2 eggs
250 ml milk
250 ml cake flour
5 ml baking powder

Preheat the oven to 180°C (350°F).

Cover the base of a greased soufflé dish with the flaked tuna. Sprinkle with first the onion and then the cheese. Do not mix. Beat the eggs and milk together. Add the flour and baking powder and beat well. Pour the mixture over the contents of the soufflé dish. Bake for about 25 minutes or until nicely browned. Serve hot.

TUNA WITH NOODLES

1 litre (4 x 250 ml) shell noodles
salt
12,5 ml cooking oil
2 cans (185 g each) savoury light-meat tuna
375 ml grated Cheddar cheese
½ packet cream of mushroom soup powder
250 ml milk
dried parsley
paprika

Boil the noodles until tender in salted water to which the cooking oil has been added. Drain. Preheat the oven to 180°C (350°F).

Meanwhile, flake the tuna and add 250 ml of the grated cheese. Mix the soup with the milk and cook until thick. Add the noodles and soup to the tuna and cheese and stir lightly. Spoon into a greased ovenproof dish. Sprinkle the rest of the cheese over and top with a sprinkling of parsley and paprika. Bake for 20 minutes or until the cheese starts to brown.

SMOORSNOEK DISH

1 large onion, chopped
30 ml margarine
1 can (400 g) smoorsnoek
750 ml cooked rice
10 ml dried parsley
salt and pepper
3 hard-boiled eggs, shelled and cut into rings
1 lemon, sliced (optional)

Fry the onion lightly in the margarine until translucent. Add the snoek, cooked rice, parsley and salt and pepper to taste. Stir well. Cover and cook for about 10 minutes over low heat. Add a little boiling water if the mixture is too dry. Reserve a few egg slices for garnishing and stir the rest into the fish mixture. Spoon onto a serving platter and garnish with egg slices, parsley and lemon slices, if desired.

Tip
This smoorsnoek dish makes an excellent starter to a meal.

FISH CAKES

1 can (425 g) pilchards in tomato sauce
1 can (200 g) tuna, drained
1 onion, grated
1 egg, beaten
10 ml dried parsley
125 ml cake flour
salt and pepper to taste

Mash the pilchards in tomato sauce and tuna. Add the rest of the ingredients and mix well.

Preheat a pan to fairly hot. Add a little oil. Drop spoonfuls of the fish mixture into the oil and fry on both sides until brown. Serve hot.

Tip

To banish fish odours, boil a little tea in the pan in which the fish was fried.

HAKE WITH YOGHURT SAUCE

1 packet (800 g) hake fillets
salt and pepper
150 ml grated Cheddar cheese
10 ml dried parsley
175 ml milk
1 packet cream of mushroom soup powder
125 ml unflavoured yoghurt

Preheat the oven to 180°C (350°F).

Season the fish with salt and pepper and arrange in a greased ovenproof dish. Sprinkle the cheese and parsley over.

Mix the milk, soup powder and yoghurt and spoon over the fish. Bake for 40 minutes or until the sauce starts to brown.

TARTAR SAUCE

15 ml sandwich spread
50 ml mayonnaise
30 ml milk
5 ml tomato sauce
3 ml flavour enhancer

Mix all the ingredients together well and serve with fish.

ERIC'S MOCK CRAYFISH

5 ml flavour enhancer
3 ml salt
3 ml black pepper
15 ml onion, finely grated
15 ml lemon juice
75 ml mayonnaise
25 ml milk
3 ml Worcester sauce
3 ml Tabasco sauce
25 ml tomato sauce
800 g hake, cooked and flaked

Mix all the ingredients thoroughly, except the fish. Stir in the fish. Serve with cold jacket potatoes and a mixed salad.

This recipe can be halved and served, on lettuce, as a starter.

Tip

Boil whole, unpeeled potatoes for 5 minutes. Remove the skins, roll in flour mixed with salt and pepper and bake until cooked.

RIGHT: Fish cakes

FISH LASAGNE

375 g spinach noodles

15 ml cooking oil

30 ml margarine

1 large onion, chopped

5 ml garlic flakes

1 can (410 g) tomato soup

125 ml water

10 ml sugar

5 ml salt

1 ml pepper

2 cans (200 g each) tuna, drained

500 ml basic white sauce*

250 ml grated Cheddar cheese

Boil the spinach noodles according to the instructions on the packet. Drain the noodles well and mix with the cooking oil.

Meanwhile, melt the margarine in a saucepan and fry the onion lightly. Add the garlic flakes, tomato soup, water, sugar, salt and pepper. Heat the mixture to boiling point, stirring occasionally, and simmer for 10 minutes over low heat. Flake the fish, stir it into the soup mixture and set aside until needed.

Meanwhile, make the white sauce. Stir in 175 ml grated cheese.

Preheat the oven to 180°C (350°F).

Spoon half the spinach noodles into a greased ovenproof dish. Spoon half the fish mixture and half the cheese sauce over. Repeat the layers with the remaining noodles, fish mixture and cheese sauce. Sprinkle the rest of the cheese on top. Bake for 30 minutes.

BAKED ASPARAGUS FISH

600 g hake

3 ml salt

3 ml coarsely ground black pepper

5 ml lemon juice

1 can (410 g) asparagus, drained

500 ml basic white sauce*

250 ml grated Cheddar cheese

125 ml dried breadcrumbs

Preheat the oven to 180°C (350°F).

Place the fish in a single layer in a greased ovenproof dish. Sprinkle the salt, pepper and lemon juice over. Arrange the asparagus on top of the fish. Pour the white sauce over and sprinkle the cheese and breadcrumbs on top. Bake for 35 minutes.

RIGHT: Eric's mock crayfish

CHICKEN FAVOURITES

You're always a winner if you prepare chicken. Today's main course becomes tomorrow's salad, or a tasty filling for sandwiches or baked potatoes.

KING ARTHUR'S CHICKEN MARINADE

1 onion, chopped
1 packet chicken marinade
30 ml tomato sauce
30 ml Worcester sauce
250 ml chutney
10 ml sugar
5 ml salt
pepper
125 ml water
15 ml cooking oil

Mix all the ingredients together. Marinate the chicken portions in the sauce for at least an hour before cooking.

APRICOT CHICKEN

6-8 chicken portions
1 packet cream of mushroom soup powder
250 ml apricot juice
125 ml cold water

Preheat the oven to 180°C (350°F).
   Roll the chicken portions in the soup powder and pack them in an ovenproof dish with a lid. Sprinkle the rest of the soup powder over the chicken. Mix the apricot juice and the water and pour over the chicken. Cover and bake for 1-1½ hours.

MICROWAVE METHOD
Microwave the chicken on 100% power for 12 minutes, then on 70% power for a further 15 minutes. Allow to stand for 5 minutes before removing the lid.

CHICKEN IN WINE

6-8 chicken portions
salt and pepper
30 ml cake flour
3 ml curry powder
1 handful seedless raisins
250 ml white wine
30 ml Worcester sauce
30 ml tomato sauce
5 ml sugar
15 ml cooking oil

Preheat the oven to 180°C (350°F).
   Season the chicken lightly with salt and pepper. Mix the flour and curry powder and roll the chicken portions in the mixture. Place the chicken in an ovenproof dish with a lid. Sprinkle the raisins over. Mix the rest of the ingredients and pour over the raisins. Cover with the lid and bake for 1-1½ hours.

> ### Tip
> *Coke, blatjang and mayonnaise makes a really delicious marinade.*

ASK-FOR-MORE CHICKEN

6-8 chicken portions

salt and pepper

125 ml seedless raisins

1 packet brown onion soup powder

250 ml boiling water

250 ml chutney

250 ml mayonnaise

Preheat the oven to 180°C (350°F).

Season the chicken with a little salt and pepper and arrange in an ovenproof dish with a lid. Sprinkle the raisins over.

Mix the soup powder and boiling water and add the rest of the ingredients. Pour the sauce over the chicken portions and cover with the lid. Bake for 1-1½ hours.

PEACH AND LATE HARVEST CHICKEN

75 ml cake flour

10 ml flavour enhancer

1 ml pepper

6-8 chicken portions

cooking oil

250 ml canned peaches, chopped

2 onions, chopped

1 chicken stock cube

200 ml boiling water

200 ml late harvest wine

50 ml medium-sweet mustard sauce

25 ml chutney

25 ml cornflour

Preheat the oven to 180°C (350°F).

Mix the flour, flavour enhancer and pepper. Roll the chicken portions in the mixture. Fry the chicken in a little oil in a frying pan until golden brown on both sides. Arrange the chicken portions in a large ovenproof dish with a lid and sprinkle the peaches over.

Sauté the onions in the same pan in which the chicken was fried. Dissolve the chicken stock cube in the boiling water. Add the wine. Mix the rest of the ingredients and stir into the chicken stock. Add to the onions and cook until thickened.

Pour the sauce over the chicken. Cover with the lid and bake for about 1½ hours.

RUM AND RAISIN CHICKEN

6-8 chicken portions

oil

1 can (410 g) tomato and onion mix

200 ml seedless raisins

2 ml cinnamon

2 ml nutmeg

3 ml paprika

2 ml rum essence

a few drops Tabasco sauce

peel and juice of ½ lemon

salt to taste

Fry the chicken portions in a little oil in a saucepan. Add the remaining ingredients and simmer until the chicken is cooked and tender.

SPANISH CHICKEN

2 onions, chopped

6-8 chicken portions

12,5 ml margarine

2 tomatoes, skinned and chopped

3 carrots, peeled and sliced

1 packet thick vegetable soup powder

500 ml water

50 ml mayonnaise

50 ml chutney

12,5 ml tomato sauce

15 ml parsley

2 bay leaves

10 ml flavour enhancer

Fry the onions and chicken lightly in the margarine in a fairly large saucepan. Add the tomatoes and carrots. Mix the rest of the ingredients and add to the chicken portions. Simmer slowly over low heat for about 1 hour or until the chicken and carrots are tender.

BARCELONA CHICKEN

6-8 chicken portions
125 g rindless shoulder bacon
125 g garlic polony
2 large onions, cut into rings
15 ml oil
125 ml tomato purée
10 ml flavour enhancer
3 ml black pepper
10 ml chutney
5 ml Worcester sauce
1 packet cream of mushroom soup powder
400 ml boiling water

Preheat the oven to 180°C (350°F).

Place the chicken portions in an ovenproof dish with a lid. Cut the bacon into thin strips, cube the garlic polony and sprinkle over the chicken. Arrange the onion rings on top of the chicken portions. Mix the oil, tomato purée, flavour enhancer, black pepper, chutney, Worcester sauce and soup powder with the boiling water and pour over the chicken. Cover with the lid and bake for 2-2½ hours.

BAKE-IN-A-BAG CHICKEN

5 ml flavour enhancer
5 ml mixed spice
5 ml paprika
125 ml dried breadcrumbs
½ packet brown onion soup powder
1 whole chicken

Preheat the oven to 180°C (350°F).

Place all the ingredients, except the chicken, in a medium baking bag. Shake well. Place the chicken in the bag and shake well. Place the bag in an ovenproof dish and fold the open end under the chicken. Bake the chicken for 1 hour. When finished baking, cut open the bag and remove it immediately. Pour all the sauce over the chicken. Switch off the oven and return the chicken to the oven for a further 5 minutes.

MICROWAVE METHOD
Follow the method to the point where the chicken is placed in the oven. Microwave the chicken on 100% power for 12 minutes, then on 70% power for a further 15 minutes. As soon as the chicken is cooked, cut the bag open and remove it.

SHERRIED CHICKEN POTJIE

6-8 chicken portions
100 g rindless bacon, cut into strips
50 g margarine
3 carrots, cut into rings
1 can (410 g) peas
4 medium potatoes, peeled and halved
250 g button mushrooms
3 ml mild curry powder
5 ml flavour enhancer
3 ml garlic powder
5 ml black pepper
125 ml sherry
1 chicken stock cube, dissolved in 300 ml boiling water

Fry the chicken and bacon in the margarine until the chicken browns. Add the vegetables to the chicken in this order: carrots, peas, potatoes and mushrooms. Mix the spices with the sherry and chicken stock and pour over the vegetables. Cover with the lid and simmer for 45-60 minutes or until the vegetables are tender.

LEFT: Bake-in-a-bag chicken

CHICKEN CURRY

5-10 ml curry powder

10 ml turmeric

25 ml margarine

2 onions, chopped

6-8 chicken portions

6 potatoes, peeled and quartered

3 carrots, peeled and sliced

250 ml shredded canned peaches

1 chicken stock cube

250 ml boiling water

50 ml chutney

12,5 ml vinegar

salt and pepper to taste

Place the curry powder and turmeric in a fairly large heavy-based saucepan and heat over low heat. Take care not to burn the curry powder. Add the margarine and fry the onions and chicken lightly in it. Place the potatoes, carrots and peaches on top of the chicken. Mix the rest of the ingredients and add. Simmer over low heat for about 1 hour or until the chicken meat starts to separate from the bone.

STIR-FRY CHICKEN

cooking oil

2 large onions, sliced

750 ml shredded cabbage

3 carrots, peeled and cut into strips

1 green pepper, cut into strips

½ English cucumber, cut into strips

1 can (440 g) pineapple chunks, drained

4 cooked halved chicken breasts, boned and cubed

salt and pepper to taste

Heat a little cooking oil in a large pan or sauce-pan. Add all the ingredients, except the chicken, and stir-fry until almost cooked. Add the chicken and season to taste with salt and pepper.

JUICY CHICKEN POTJIE

Although this dish should be made in a black cast-iron pot over the coals, it tastes just as good if you use a heavy-based saucepan and cook it on top of the stove.

6-8 chicken portions

cooking oil for frying

3 onions, quartered

3 carrots, peeled and sliced into rings

250 ml shredded green beans

250 g young baby marrows, halved lengthways

10 small potatoes, peeled

1 packet brown onion soup powder

25 ml chutney

5 ml paprika

12,5 ml Worcester sauce

25 ml mayonnaise

125 ml dry white wine

salt and pepper

Fry the chicken in the oil until lightly browned. Reduce the heat and add the vegetables in the following order: onions, carrots, green beans, baby marrows, and potatoes. Mix the rest of the ingredients and pour over the vegetables. Cover with the lid and simmer for 1-1½ hours. If the mixture gets too dry, add a little more water.

RIGHT: Stir-fry chicken

CAPE PEAR CHICKEN

6-8 chicken portions

250 ml pear juice

60 ml mayonnaise

5 ml sherry or sweet wine

10 ml fruit chutney

3 ml flavour enhancer

3 ml black pepper

5 ml paprika

Preheat the oven to 180°C (350°F).

Place the chicken portions in an ovenproof dish with a lid. Mix the pear juice, mayonnaise, sherry or sweet wine and chutney together well and pour over the chicken. Sprinkle the flavour enhancer and pepper over, and lastly the paprika. Cover with the lid and bake for 30 minutes. Remove the lid and bake the chicken for a further 30 minutes.

CHICKEN STEW

1 whole chicken

salt and pepper

1 packet cream of mushroom soup powder

250 ml macaroni pieces

125 g margarine

2 medium onions, chopped

4 medium tomatoes, skinned and chopped

125 ml cake flour

200 ml water

250 g Cheddar cheese, grated

Season the chicken with salt and pepper and cook in a little water until tender. Remove the chicken from the saucepan, bone it and cube the flesh. Make the chicken stock in the saucepan up to 625 ml with water. Add the soup powder and cook until thick. Stir often.

Meanwhile, boil the macaroni pieces in salted water until soft and drain.

Melt the margarine in a large saucepan and add the onions. Sauté until soft. Add the tomatoes and cook for a few minutes. Take care not to burn them. Mix the flour with the water and stir it into the tomato mixture. Add the soup and mix. Add the chicken, cheese and macaroni, stir lightly and simmer for 12 minutes.

CHICKEN À LA KING

1 whole chicken

2 onions, chopped

1 green pepper, chopped

2 tomatoes, skinned and chopped

25 ml margarine

100 ml chicken stock

1 packet cream of mushroom soup powder

1 packet cream of chicken soup powder

700 ml milk

12,5 ml chutney

10 ml brandy or sherry

Cook the chicken until done. Reserve 100 ml chicken stock. Remove the skin and bones from the chicken and cube the meat.

Meanwhile, fry the onions, green pepper and tomatoes in the margarine in a fairly large saucepan until soft. Mix the chicken stock with the soup, milk and chutney and add to the onion mixture. Simmer for about 10 minutes until the mixture is thick and cooked. Add the chicken and simmer for a few minutes. Stir in the brandy or sherry and serve hot.

Tip

Use a potato masher to mix flour and butter. This saves a lot of time.

RIGHT: Juicy chicken potjie

CHICKEN À LA MADELEIN

1 whole chicken
2 carrots, peeled and cut into rings
3 ml coarsely ground black pepper
500 ml water
1 small onion, cut into rings
5 ml flavour enhancer

SAUCE

125 ml butter or margarine
125 ml cake flour
500 ml stock (from cooked chicken)
125 g button mushrooms, sliced
60 ml chopped green pepper
1 can (410 g) peas
1 ml peri-peri
5 ml flavour enhancer
3 ml coarsely ground black pepper
30 ml sherry
250 ml cream

Cook the chicken and all the other ingredients together until tender. Remove the skin and bones and cut the meat into cubes or strips. Reserve the chicken stock in which the chicken was cooked.

Melt the butter or margarine in a saucepan large enough to take all the ingredients. Stir in the flour and add the stock, stirring briskly. Add all the other ingredients, except the cream, and cook over low heat until the vegetables are soft. Stir in the chicken and simmer for a further 10 minutes. Stir in the cream just before serving.

SWEET AND TANGY CHICKEN

6-8 chicken portions
125 ml mayonnaise
125 ml smooth apricot jam
5 ml flavour enhancer
5 ml paprika

Preheat the oven to 180°C (350°F).

Place the chicken in an ovenproof dish. Mix the mayonnaise and apricot jam and spoon it over the chicken portions. Sprinkle the flavour enhancer and paprika over the chicken and bake, uncovered, for 1¼ hours or until the chicken is tender.

Tip

Keep a transparent plastic bag in your recipe book. Place the open recipe book in it while you're working and the book will remain clean.

RANDSAVER MINCE

You can concoct wonderful dishes with economical mince and a little imagination; not to mention old favourites like bobotie and lasagne.

LASAGNE

300 g spinach noodles
2 onions, chopped
1 green pepper, finely chopped
1 clove garlic, crushed
10 ml oil
750 g lean mince
2 cans (115 g each) tomato paste
10 ml sugar
150 ml boiling water
5 ml oregano
1,5 ml thyme
5 ml coarsely ground black pepper
5 ml flavour enhancer
60 ml chutney
500 ml basic white sauce*
190 ml grated Cheddar cheese

Boil the noodles until tender according to the instructions on the packet, and drain.

Preheat the oven to 180°C (350°F).

Fry the onions, green pepper and garlic in the oil until soft but not brown. Add the mince and fry over moderate heat until done. Mix the tomato paste and sugar with the boiling water and stir into the meat mixture. Add the herbs, spices and chutney. Increase the heat and cook for 3 minutes. Layer the noodles, meat and white sauce in a greased ovenproof dish. End with white sauce and sprinkle the cheese over.

Bake for 25-30 minutes. Serve hot.

RINA'S LASAGNE

1 packet (500 g) spinach noodles
25 ml cooking oil
2 onions, chopped
25 ml margarine
1 kg mince
salt and pepper
2 cans (115 g each) tomato paste
60 ml sugar
2 packets mushroom sauce powder
500 ml milk
1 litre (4 x 250 ml) basic white sauce*
250 ml grated Cheddar cheese
2 eggs

Boil the noodles until soft in salted water to which the oil has been added. Drain and set aside. Preheat the oven to 180°C (350°F).

Fry the onions in the margarine. Add the mince and stir until almost cooked. Add salt and pepper to taste. Mix the tomato paste with the sugar and add to the meat. Stir well. Mix the sauce powder with 250 ml of the milk. Add to the mince mixture and stir.

Grease two ovenproof dishes. Spoon a layer of spinach noodles into the dishes, followed by a layer each of mince, white sauce and cheese. Repeat the layers. Beat the eggs with the rest of the milk and pour over the top. Bake for 30 minutes or until golden brown. Serve hot.

Allow one of the dishes to cool, cover and freeze for later use.

REEKS'S SPAGHETTI BOLOGNAISE

1 packet (500 g) spaghetti

1 green pepper, finely chopped

2 onions, sliced into rings

100 g rindless shoulder bacon, cut into strips

30 ml oil

20 ml margarine

500 g lean mince

200 ml tomato purée

30 ml fruit chutney

150 ml water

5 ml black pepper

5 ml oregano

5 ml garlic flakes

250 ml button mushrooms, sliced

Boil the spaghetti according to the instructions on the packet. Drain and keep warm.

Meanwhile, fry the green pepper, onions and bacon in a mixture of the oil and margarine until cooked. Add the mince and fry over low heat, stirring often. Mix the tomato purée, chutney and water and add to the meat. Sprinkle the black pepper, oregano and garlic flakes over and stir well. Add the mushrooms and cook for 30 minutes over moderate heat. Serve with the spaghetti and a mixed salad.

SPAGHETTI BOLOGNAISE

¾ packet (375 g) spaghetti

1 onion, finely chopped

12,5 ml margarine

500 g mince

5 ml salt

3 ml mixed spice

3 ml thyme

3 ml cinnamon

12,5 ml apricot jam

25 ml chutney

1 can (410 g) tomato purée

grated Cheddar cheese

Boil the spaghetti according to the instructions on the packet. Drain and keep warm.

Meanwhile, fry the finely chopped onion lightly in the margarine in a saucepan until golden brown. Add the mince and cook until done. Stir from time to time to ensure that the mince does not get lumpy. Add the rest of the ingredients, except the grated cheese. Stir well and cook for a further 10 minutes over low heat.

Serve as follows: Spoon hot cooked spaghetti onto each plate and spoon the mince sauce on top. Sprinkle a little grated cheese over.

FRIKKADELS

1 kg mince

2 slices white bread, soaked in water and well drained

2 onions, grated

2 carrots, peeled and finely grated

2 potatoes, peeled and finely grated

1 packet oxtail soup powder

100 ml milk

12,5 ml vinegar

salt and pepper to taste (remember the soup powder is salty)

Preheat the oven to 180°C (350°F).

Mix all the ingredients well. Roll the mixture into balls and pack them in a greased roasting pan. Bake for about 25 minutes. Do not cover the frikkadels. Turn over after the first 15 minutes.

WRAPPED FRIKKADELS

single quantity frikkadels*, cooked and cooled

250 g bacon rashers

Wrap a bacon rasher around each frikkadel and secure with a cocktail stick.

Braai over the coals or under the grill until the bacon is cooked and crisp.

RIGHT: Wrapped frikkadels

CURRIED FRIKKADELS

single quantity frikkadels*, uncooked

2 onions, chopped

60 ml butter or margarine

30 ml cake flour

250 ml water

30 ml sugar

5 ml flavour enhancer

3 ml black pepper

1 ml cayenne pepper

5 ml turmeric

30 ml mild curry powder

3 bananas, sliced

30 ml apricot jam

Preheat the oven to 180°C (350°F).
Place the frikkadels in a greased ovenproof dish.
Make a sauce from the rest of the ingredients:
Fry the onions in the butter or margarine until
translucent and stir in the flour. Add all the other
ingredients and cook over moderate heat until
the bananas break into pieces down. Pour the
hot sauce over the frikkadels and bake for
40 minutes.

COTTAGE PIE

5 large potatoes, peeled

1 onion

15 ml cooking oil

500 g mince

1 small can (225 g) mixed vegetables, drained

12,5 ml chutney

pepper

1 packet cream of mushroom soup powder

125 ml cold water

12,5 ml margarine

200 ml milk

5 ml baking powder

pinch of salt

2 ml nutmeg

1 egg, beaten with 12,5 ml milk

paprika (optional)

Preheat the oven to 180°C (350°F).
 Boil the potatoes in water until soft, or microwave on 100% power for 12 minutes.
 Meanwhile, fry the onion in oil until translucent. Add the mince, mixed vegetables, chutney
and pepper. Mix the soup powder with the cold
water and add to the mince mixture. Stir well
and cover with the lid. Cook for 20-25 minutes or
until done. Stir from time to time. If the mixture
gets too dry, add a little boiling water. Spoon the
mince mixture into a greased ovenproof dish
and set aside.
 Mash the cooked potatoes and add the
margarine and milk. Mix well. Add the baking
powder, salt and nutmeg. Mix well.
 Spoon the potato mixture over the meat
mixture and smooth the top.
 Pour the egg and milk mixture over the
potatoes and sprinkle a little paprika over, if
desired. Bake for about 25 minutes or until
browned.

MINCE SURPRISE

500 g mince

1 onion, chopped

1 small can (225 g) mixed vegetables, drained

250 ml uncooked rice

1 can (410 g) minestrone

500 ml boiling water

salt to taste

50 ml tomato sauce mixed with 5 ml curry powder

Preheat the oven to 180°C (350°F).
 Place the mince in a saucepan and stir over
moderate heat until the grains are separate but
not cooked. Place the mince in a fairly deep
3 litre ovenproof dish with a lid. Layer in the rest
of the ingredients, in the order given.
Cover and bake for 45-60 minutes or until the
rice is cooked.

MINCE CURRY

1 large onion, chopped

12,5 ml cooking oil

10 ml mild curry powder

5 ml turmeric

25 ml chutney

25 ml vinegar

5 ml sugar

3 ml salt

500 g mince

2 carrots, finely grated

1 green apple, coarsely grated

125 ml water

2 large potatoes, cubed

½ packet brown onion soup powder

Fry the onion slowly in the cooking oil for 5 minutes. Add the curry and turmeric and stir to mix. Add the chutney, vinegar, sugar and salt and simmer slowly for 10 minutes. Add the mince and finely grated carrots. Stir until the meat grains are separate. Add the apple and water and simmer for 20 minutes. Stir from time to time to prevent burning.

Meanwhile, boil the potatoes until soft in water to which 3 ml turmeric has been added. Drain and add the potatoes to the meat.

Mix the soup with 75 ml water and add to the meat. Cook for 10 minutes.

TOMATO MINCE

1 onion, chopped

12,5 ml cooking oil

500 g mince

125 ml breadcrumbs

60 ml tomato sauce

1 egg, beaten

2 ml mixed herbs

salt and pepper to taste

250 ml grated Cheddar cheese

Preheat the oven to 200°C (400°F).

Fry the onion lightly in the oil until cooked. Add the mince and stir until the grains separate and the red colour disappears. Remove from the stove and add the other ingredients. Stir well.

Spoon into a greased ovenproof dish and bake for 25 minutes.

BOBOTIE

GROUP A

20 ml ground ginger

30 ml soft brown sugar

10 ml curry powder

15 ml turmeric

10 ml salt

1 ml pepper

60 ml margarine

5 medium onions, chopped

GROUP B

2 slices white bread, soaked in water

1 kg lean mince

150 ml seedless raisins

60 ml chutney

30 ml smooth apricot jam

30 ml vinegar

30 ml Worcester sauce

30 ml tomato paste

GROUP C

375 ml milk

2 eggs

fresh lemon leaves or bay leaves

Heat all the dry ingredients in Group A in a heavy-based saucepan. Take care not to burn them. Add the margarine and onions and sauté until the onions are soft.

Preheat the oven to 180°C (350°F).

Squeeze the water from the bread and stir all the ingredients in Group B into the onion mixture. Cook for 20 minutes over low heat, stirring from time to time. Spoon the mixture into a greased ovenproof dish.

Beat the milk and eggs together and pour over the meat. Press a few lemon or bay leaves into the mixture and bake for 45 minutes. Serve hot.

FRUITY BOBOTIE

2 slices brown bread

200 ml milk

2 onions, finely chopped

25 ml oil

25 ml lemon juice

8 ml curry powder

5 ml turmeric

5 ml flavour enhancer

2 ml pepper

500 g lean mince

30 ml chutney

2 eggs

125 ml chopped dried apricots

1 green apple, grated

75 ml seedless raisins

Preheat the oven to 180°C (350°F).

Soak the bread in the milk. Fry the onions in the oil and add the lemon juice. Stir in the curry powder, turmeric, flavour enhancer and pepper. Squeeze the milk from the bread and reserve the milk. Add the bread to the onion mixture. Add the meat, chutney, 1 egg, apricots, grated apple and raisins and cook for 20 minutes over low heat. Stir from time to time.

Spoon the mixture into a greased ovenproof dish. Mix the remaining egg with the reserved milk and pour over the meat mixture. Bake for 30 minutes.

COEN 'S MINCE POTJIE

750 g mince

cooking oil

salt and pepper

4 large onions, chopped

250 g bacon, shredded

250 g uncooked rice

250 g button mushrooms (optional)

1 can (425 g) cream of mushroom soup

1 can (410 g) ravioli

Fry the mince lightly in a little oil. (The saucepan should merely be brushed with oil.) Add salt and pepper to taste. Add the rest of the ingredients in the order in which they are given. Cover with the lid and cook slowly for 45 minutes. Check from time to time that the mince is not burning, but do not stir – the dish looks like a cake with a number of layers.

LEFT: Bobotie

FOR THE MEAT EATERS

Red meat is expensive, but this doesn't mean that it has to disappear from the menu. We paid special attention to these meat recipes to make them both economical and flavourful.

MOCK VENISON

2 kg stewing beef, trimmed of fat
100 g speck, shredded
75 ml vinegar
75 ml Worcester sauce
15 ml salt
10 cloves
50 ml water
black pepper

Place all the ingredients in a pressure cooker and pressure-cook for 50 minutes until the meat falls off the bone. Remove the bones and chop the meat finely. Remove the pressure gauge and simmer for 15 minutes.

MOCK VENISON PIE

mock venison* (recipe above)

QUICK PIE CRUST
1 egg
125 ml milk
125 ml cooking oil
375 ml cake flour
7 ml baking powder
pinch of salt

Prepare the mock venison and spoon into a greased pie dish.
Preheat the oven to 200°C (400°F).
Prepare the crust: Beat the egg, milk and oil together. Beat in the dry ingredients, a little at a time. Spoon over the meat and bake for about 20 minutes or until browned.

STEAK IN WINE

4-6 fillet steaks
125 ml dry red wine
125 ml cake flour
5 ml flavour enhancer
5 ml coarsely ground black pepper
5 ml oregano
5 ml garlic powder
125 ml oil
30 g margarine

Preheat the oven to 180°C (350°F).
Place the fillet steaks in an ovenproof dish and pour the red wine over. Cover and bake for 20 minutes. Remove from the oven and allow to cool.
Mix the flour, flavour enhancer, black pepper, oregano and garlic powder and roll the meat in it. Heat the oil and margarine and fry the meat in a frying pan until brown, or to personal taste.

Tip
Friends and family will be very impressed if you prepare Mock Venison Pie in individual bowls.

MELT-IN-THE-MOUTH STEAK

1 kg tenderised steak

cake flour

salt and pepper

cooking oil

SAUCE

15 ml cake flour

15 ml flavour enhancer

37,5 ml tomato sauce

12,5 ml vinegar

12,5 ml Worcester sauce

750 ml water

Preheat the oven to 160°C (325°F).
Roll the steak in flour and sprinkle with salt and pepper. Shallow-fry in oil on both sides until browned. Place in an ovenproof dish with a lid. Mix all the sauce ingredients together and stir over low heat until boiling point is reached. Boil for 5 minutes.
Pour the sauce over the meat and cover with the lid. Bake for 2 hours.

ALL-TIME FAVOURITE BEEF

1 kg tenderised beef, cut into strips

75 g margarine

15 ml oil

1 large onion, chopped

250 g button mushrooms, sliced

50 ml cake flour

450 ml hot water

5 ml flavour enhancer

3 ml garlic powder

5 ml coarsely ground black pepper

15 ml paprika

5 ml peri-peri

200 ml cream

Fry the meat in a mixture of margarine and oil in a heavy-based saucepan. Add the onion and mushrooms and sauté for 6-8 minutes. Sprinkle the flour over and stir well. Add the hot water and stir often until the mixture boils. Stir in the spices. Cover with the lid and simmer for 1 hour.
Remove from the stove and add the cream just before serving.

CURRY AND RICE

750 g stewing beef, cubed

125 ml cake flour

30 ml oil

50 g margarine

2 onions, cut into rings

400 ml boiling water

125 ml sultanas

30 ml coconut

5 ml flavour enhancer

3 ml garlic powder

3 ml masala

15 ml mild curry powder

5 ml black pepper

3 ml ground cumin

20 ml lemon juice

60 ml fruit chutney

Roll the meat in the flour. Heat the oil and margarine and fry the meat and onions. Pour 350 ml boiling water over the meat and stir in the sultanas and coconut.
Mix all the spices well and add the lemon juice and chutney. Add 50 ml boiling water to the spices and stir well before stirring into the meat. Simmer for about 1½ hours over low heat, or until the meat is very tender.
Serve with rice, chutney, finely chopped onions and tomato.

OXTAIL STEW

15 ml margarine

2 onions, cut into rings

1,25 kg oxtail

6 medium potatoes, peeled and halved

125 ml boiling water

30 ml fruit chutney

30 ml tomato sauce

30 ml honey

60 ml white vinegar

10 ml mild curry powder

3 ml black pepper

5 ml flavour enhancer

Melt the margarine in a pressure cooker without the lid and fry the onions until cooked. Add the meat and pressure-cook for 50 minutes. Add the potatoes. Mix all the other ingredients, except the spices, and add to the meat. Lastly, sprinkle the spices over. Pressure-cook for a further 15 minutes. Simmer, without pressure, for 20 minutes until the meat and potatoes are tender. Serve hot with rice.

TIPSY LAMB POTJIE

2 large onions, cut into rings

100 g margarine

1,25 kg lamb knuckles

150 ml sweet wine

15 ml brandy

10 ml flavour enhancer

3 ml black pepper

3 ml ground coriander

4-6 potatoes, peeled and quartered

250 g carrots, cut into rings

250 g button mushrooms, rinsed and halved

250 g baby marrows, cut into rings

Fry the onions in the margarine and add the lamb knuckles. Fry over low heat for 5 minutes. Add the sweet wine, brandy and spices. Cover with the lid and cook for 45 minutes or until the meat starts to soften. Add the vegetables, packing them in layers on top of the meat. Cover again and cook for a further 30 minutes over moderate heat or until the vegetables are tender.

This potjie can be cooked on the stove or in a cast-iron pot over the coals.

LAMB CURRY

10 ml curry powder

3 ml ground ginger

15 ml turmeric

25 ml margarine

3 large onions, chopped

1 green pepper, chopped

8-10 lamb neck chops

50 ml chutney

25 ml apricot jam

12,5 ml vinegar

5 ml sugar

10 ml salt

250 ml water

3 bay leaves

4 carrots, cubed or cut into rings

1 can (410 g) peas

6 potatoes, peeled and quartered

1 can (420 g) beans in tomato sauce

custard powder mixed to a paste with water (optional)

Set the stove plate on moderate. Place the curry powder, ginger and turmeric in a pressure cooker and place, uncovered, on the stove. Heat until just warm – take care that it doesn't burn. Add the margarine and fry the onions and green pepper lightly. Add the chops. Mix the chutney, jam, vinegar, sugar, salt and water and add to the meat. Add the bay leaves. Cover with the lid and pressure-cook for 30 minutes.

Add the carrots, peas and potatoes and pressure-cook for a further 15 minutes. Remove the pressure gauge and add the beans. Simmer for 15 minutes. If the sauce is too thin, mix a little custard powder with water and add.

LEFT: Mock venison pie

LAMB NECK CASSEROLE

1,25 kg lamb neck chops

2 onions, cut into rings

30 ml oil

10 ml flavour enhancer

3 ml black pepper

50 g dried apricots, chopped

250 ml hot meat stock

Preheat the oven to 180°C (350°F).

Fry the meat and onions in oil until golden brown. Spoon the meat and onions into an ovenproof dish and add all the other ingredients. Cover with a lid and bake for 1½ hours.

FRUITY LAMB POTJIE

1 beef stock cube

250 ml boiling water

250 ml dried apricots

15 ml sugar

1 kg lamb shank, sliced

15 ml cooking oil

3 large onions, sliced

1 large ripe tomato, skinned and sliced

250 g young baby marrows, halved lengthways

6 potatoes, peeled and quartered

250 g button mushrooms

2 ml black pepper

10 ml salt

2 ml oregano

1 ml ground cloves

5 ml garlic flakes

2 ml paprika

Dissolve the stock cube in the boiling water and pour over the dried apricots. Add the sugar and set aside for 15 minutes.

In an uncovered pressure cooker, fry the lamb shank slices in hot oil until browned. Add the onions and sauté until translucent. Add the apricots and stock. Cover the pressure cooker with the lid and pressure-cook for 25 minutes.

Add the rest of the ingredients and simmer for about 50 minutes, without pressure, until the vegetables are tender.

PAPRIKA LAMB CHOPS

6-8 lamb leg chops

1 large onion, cut into rings

1 green pepper, cut into strips

30 ml oil

3 ml salt

3 ml coarsely ground black pepper

15 ml paprika

10 ml cake flour

150 ml meat stock

125 ml tomato purée

125 ml evaporated milk

Preheat the oven to 180°C (350°F).

Fry the meat, onion and green pepper in oil until browned. Mix the spices and flour and sprinkle over the meat. Fry for a further 2 minutes and spoon the chops into an ovenproof dish. Mix the meat stock and tomato purée and pour over the meat. Cover and bake for 1 hour. Add the evaporated milk and bake for a further 10 minutes, uncovered.

VIRGINIA'S PORK CHOPS

6-8 pork chops

3 eggs, beaten

150 ml cake flour

10 ml flavour enhancer

5 ml coarsely ground black pepper

cooking oil

Dip the chops in the egg. Mix the flour and spices and roll the meat in it. Heat the oil and fry the meat until golden brown and cooked.

RIGHT: Festive pork chops

SWEET-AND-SOUR PORK

750 g pork fillet, cubed

75 ml butter or margarine

5 ml flavour enhancer

1 can (825 g) pineapple chunks

100 ml boiling water

15 ml sugar

100 ml white vinegar

30 ml soy sauce

20 ml cornflour

1 green pepper, cut into strips

Fry the meat in butter or margarine until golden brown and cooked. Sprinkle with the flavour enhancer.

   Drain the pineapple chunks and mix the pineapple syrup with the boiling water, sugar, vinegar, soy sauce and cornflour. Cook over low heat for about 15 minutes, or until the sauce starts to thicken. Mix the pineapple chunks and green pepper with the sauce and pour over the pork cubes. Serve hot.

FESTIVE PORK CHOPS

6 pork chops

25 ml cake flour

pepper to taste

cooking oil

1 small can (225 g) apricots

1 packet brown onion soup powder

1 carton (250 ml) apricot juice

Preheat the oven to 180°C (350°F).

   Roll the pork chops in the flour to which pepper to taste has been added. Shallow-fry the pork chops in the oil until brown on both sides and arrange in a fairly large ovenproof dish. Spoon the apricots and 30 ml of the syrup over the pork chops. Mix the soup powder and apricot juice and pour over the apricots. Bake for 1½-2 hours or until done.

> ### Tip
> *Precook sausages in a little water until almost done. Dry with a paper towel, roll in flour and fry in hot oil.*

DESSERTS

Cool delights

Some of these recipes have been favourites since Grandma's time, when bazaar tables groaned under the weight of cold puddings.

ICE-CREAM SURPRISE

250 ml cream

meringues

vanilla ice cream

4 ripe firm bananas, sliced

1 Peppermint Crisp, grated

Whip the cream until stiff. Break the meringues into small pieces and fold into the cream.

Place a scoop of ice cream in each dish. Arrange the banana slices around the ice cream. Spoon the cream mixture over the ice cream and sprinkle with the grated Peppermint Crisp.

CHOCOLATE SPONGE PUDDING

250 ml sugar

3 eggs, separated

1 packet red jelly powder

1 litre boiling water

37,5 ml cocoa

30 ml custard powder

125 ml cold water

Mix 125 ml sugar with the egg yolks and set aside. Add the jelly powder to 500 ml boiling water and stir until the powder has dissolved. Set aside.

Mix the cocoa, custard powder, remaining sugar and cold water. Add to the remaining boiling water and cook until the mixture starts to thicken. Stir constantly.

Stir in the egg yolk and sugar mixture and cook slowly for 2 minutes. Remove from the stove and stir in the jelly mixture. Allow to cool for a few minutes. Whisk the egg whites until stiff and fold into the mixture.

Allow to set and serve cold with custard.

ITALIAN CREAM PUDDING

1 packet lemon jelly powder

pinch of salt

250 ml boiling water

750 ml milk

125 ml sugar

20 ml custard powder

3 eggs, separated

Mix the jelly powder and salt with the boiling water until dissolved and set aside on the stove to keep it warm. Make the custard with the milk, sugar and custard powder.

Meanwhile, whisk the egg whites until stiff and beat the egg yolks. When the custard is ready, remove it from the stove and quickly stir in the egg yolks. Return to the stove and stir in the warm jelly. Simmer for a minute. Remove from the stove and fold in the egg whites with a metal spoon. Pour into a serving dish and allow to cool. Place in the refrigerator until ice cold.

> ### Tip
> *For a festive touch, why not serve fresh fruit salad topped with yoghurt in beautiful glasses?*

CREAMY WHIP

1 packet jelly powder (any flavour)
250 ml boiling water
1 can (410 g) evaporated milk, chilled overnight in the refrigerator

Dissolve the jelly powder in the boiling water and allow to cool.
   Beat the evaporated milk until stiff. Add the cooled jelly and mix well. Refrigerate for at least an hour.

STRAWBERRY PUDDING

1 packet strawberry jelly powder
250 ml boiling water
250 ml evaporated milk, chilled overnight in the refrigerator
20 ml sugar
30 ml smooth strawberry jam

Dissolve the jelly powder in the boiling water and allow to cool. Whisk the evaporated milk until stiff and mix in the jelly and the remaining ingredients. Beat for at least 5 minutes. Place in the refrigerator to set.

MADELEIN 'S COLD PUDDING

1 can (410 g) evaporated milk
20 ml gelatine
125 ml boiling water
60 ml apricot jam

Place the unopened can of evaporated milk in a saucepan and cover with boiling water. Boil for 30 minutes, remove from the water and allow to cool. Leave in the refrigerator overnight.
   Dissolve the gelatine in the boiling water and allow to cool. Pour the evaporated milk into a dish and beat it until stiff. Add the jam and cooled gelatine and mix well.
Place in the refrigerator to set. Serve with canned fruit.

JELLY SNOW

1 packet jelly powder (any flavour)
250 ml boiling water
250 ml ice cubes

Dissolve the jelly powder in the boiling water and set aside for 15 minutes to cool slightly. Place the ice cubes in the jelly, one at a time, and beat quickly until the ice cubes have melted. There will be a foam layer on the jelly. Place in the refrigerator immediately to set.

BANANA JELLY

1 packet jelly powder (any flavour)
2 ripe bananas, sliced

Prepare the jelly according to the instructions on the packet. Add the banana slices and allow to set in the refrigerator.

JELLY CUSTARD

1 packet jelly powder (any flavour)
500 ml boiling water
pinch of salt
37,5 ml custard powder

Mix the jelly powder with the boiling water in a saucepan over low heat and add the salt. Mix the custard powder with a little cold water and stir into the jelly mixture. Stir the mixture until it boils. Pour into a dish and allow to cool. Place in the refrigerator until the jelly has set.

> ### Tip
> *To make jelly set quicker, add a pinch of bicarbonate of soda.*

GUAVA FRIDGE TART

1 large can (820 g) guavas, drained (reserve syrup) and shredded

1 packet red jelly powder

1 can (410 g) evaporated milk, chilled overnight in the refrigerator

2 packets Tennis biscuits

whipped cream (optional)

Pour the guava syrup into a saucepan and allow to boil briskly. Remove from the stove and add the jelly powder. Stir well until dissolved and allow to cool slightly.

Meanwhile, whip the evaporated milk until thick. Add the cooled guava syrup mixture and mix well.

Pack a layer of biscuits in a rectangular dish, then a layer of guavas and lastly a layer of milk mixture. Repeat the layers. Sprinkle biscuit crumbs over or decorate with whipped cream, if desired.

GRANADILLA FRIDGE TART

CRUST

½ packet Tennis biscuits, crushed

2 ml ground cinnamon

7 ml sugar

25 ml margarine, melted

BOTTOM LAYER

10 ml sugar

1 small can (115 g) granadilla pulp

10 ml custard powder

water

FILLING

5 ml gelatine

12,5 ml cold water

1 packet granadilla or lemon jelly powder

125 ml boiling water

350 ml granadilla yoghurt

125 ml fresh cream

Mix the biscuit crumbs, cinnamon and sugar. Add the melted margarine and mix well. Press into the base and sides of a round pie dish.

Add the sugar to the granadilla pulp and heat over moderate heat. Mix the custard powder with a little water and add. Cook until the mixture thickens. Spread over the crust and allow to cool.

Mix the gelatine with the cold water and add the jelly powder and boiling water. Stir well until the jelly powder has dissolved. Allow to cool slightly. Add the jelly to the yoghurt and then add the lightly whipped cream. Stir well and spoon over the bottom layer. Crumble a Tennis biscuit and sprinkle over (optional). Allow to set in the refrigerator.

MARSHMALLOW FRIDGE TART

½ packet Marie biscuits

20 marshmallows, shredded

10 glacé cherries, halved

4 bananas, mashed

1 can (410 g) evaporated milk, chilled overnight in the refrigerator

Pack the Marie biscuits in the base and up the sides of a rectangular pie dish. Mix the shredded marshmallows with the cherries and banana. Whip the evaporated milk until stiff and mix all together. Spoon the mixture on top of the Marie biscuits. Place in the refrigerator until ice cold and set.

CATHERINE'S COTTAGE CHEESE TART

CRUST

½ packet Marie biscuits, crushed

50 ml margarine, melted

37,5 ml sugar

FILLING

1 can (385 g) pears, drained

2 packets Orley-Whip or 250 ml fresh cream

250 g smooth cottage cheese

25 ml instant pudding powder, vanilla flavour

Mix all the crust ingredients together and press into the base and sides of a pie dish.

Arrange the pears on top of the crust.

Beat the Orley-Whip or cream until stiff. Beat the cottage cheese and instant pudding powder into the cream until well mixed. Spoon the cottage cheese mixture over the pears. Crumble a Marie biscuit and sprinkle it over the tart. Chill for 1-2 hours before serving.

LEFT: Lemon custard tart

KAREN'S PINEAPPLE TART

1 packet pineapple jelly powder

250 ml boiling water

1 can (397 g) condensed milk

1 can (440 g) crushed pineapple, drained

1 packet Tennis biscuits

Dissolve the jelly powder in the boiling water and allow to cool. Add the condensed milk and pineapple and stir well. Pack the biscuits in the base and up the sides of a rectangular pie dish. Pour the mixture into the dish. Crumble a biscuit and sprinkle over the tart. Allow to set in the refrigerator.

LEMON CUSTARD TART

1 packet Tennis biscuits

milk

500 ml thick, hot custard

125 ml lemon juice

1 can (397 g) condensed milk

250 ml cream

Dip the biscuits in the milk, one by one, and pack in a single layer in the base of a rectangular pie dish. Pour the hot custard over the biscuits. Reserve two of the remaining biscuits and crumble the rest of the biscuits. Sprinkle over the custard. Allow to cool.

Stir the lemon juice into the condensed milk until the milk thickens and spoon over the custard. Whip the cream until stiff and spread over the tart. Crush the remaining two biscuits and sprinkle over the cream.
Refrigerate until ice cold.

> ### Tip
>
> *A delightful instant pudding: Drain crushed pineapple and mix lightly with stiffly whipped cream. Spoon onto slices of hot gingerbread.*

TRIFLE

1 trifle sponge

apricot jam

1 can (410 g) fruit salad

125 ml chopped walnuts (optional)

150 ml sweet wine

1,25 litres cooked custard, cooled

1 packet red jelly, prepared and set

1 packet green jelly, prepared and set

250 ml cream, stiffly whipped

Cut the trifle sponge into 1 cm thick slices and spread a thin layer of apricot jam on each. Sandwich them together in pairs, then cube them and pack in the base of a fairly large, deep dish. Add the fruit and sprinkle the chopped nuts over (reserve a few for decoration). Mix the sweet wine with the custard and pour over the fruit. Stir the set jelly with a fork and spoon half over the custard – use both colours. Spread the stiffly whipped cream over and decorate with the remaining jelly and chopped walnuts.

Warm for winter

Spoil your family with these delectable hot puddings on cold winter evenings.

BAKED APPLES

500 ml water

200 ml sugar

2 cloves

2 pieces stick cinnamon

30 ml custard powder

6 red apples, peeled and cored

200 ml sultanas

3 ml ground cinnamon

1,5 ml ground ginger

Preheat the oven to 180°C (350°F).

Boil the water, sugar, cloves and stick cinnamon together for 15 minutes. Mix the custard powder with a little water and stir into the boiling water mixture to thicken it. Pour the sauce into an ovenproof dish just large enough to contain the apples. Place the apples in the sauce and fill the hollows with sultanas.

Sprinkle any remaining sultanas, and the cinnamon and ginger, over the apples. Bake for 1 hour. Serve with custard or ice cream.

QUICK GINGER PUDDING

1 can (410 g) pears, drained (reserve 75 ml syrup)

1½ packets ginger biscuits

1 can (410 g) evaporated milk

Preheat the oven to 180°C (350°F).

Arrange the pears in a rectangular pie dish. Break the biscuits into small pieces and sprinkle over the pears. Pour first the pear syrup and then the evaporated milk over. Ensure that all the biscuits absorb a little of the milk. Bake for 25-30 minutes or until the biscuits start to brown. Serve lukewarm.

> ### Tip
> *When measuring golden syrup or honey, brush the measuring spoon or cup with a little oil to ensure that the syrup or honey will run out easily.*

RIGHT: Baked apples

ANDRIETTE'S VINEGAR PUDDING WITH RUM SAUCE

1 egg

125 ml sugar

250 ml cake flour

5 ml baking powder

pinch of salt

5 ml bicarbonate of soda

180 ml hot milk

18 ml vinegar

12,5 ml apricot jam

SAUCE

250 ml sugar

125 ml boiling water

250 ml cream

12,5 ml margarine

5 ml rum essence

Preheat the oven to 190°C (375°F).

Beat the egg and sugar until creamy. Sift the flour, baking powder and salt together. Dissolve the bicarbonate of soda in the hot milk and add it to the flour alternately with the egg mixture. Add the vinegar and apricot jam and mix well. Spoon into a greased ovenproof dish and bake for about 35 minutes.

Boil all the sauce ingredients, except the essence. Remove from the stove and add the essence. Pour the boiling sauce over the pudding as soon as it comes from the oven. Serve with custard or ice cream.

APPLE TART WITH SULTANAS

125 ml margarine

125 ml sugar

1 egg

pinch of salt

250 ml self-raising flour

125 ml milk

1 can (410 g) pie apples, finely chopped

a handful of sultanas

cinnamon sugar

SAUCE

37,5 ml golden syrup or honey

37,5 ml margarine or butter

Preheat the oven to 190°C (375°F).

Cream the margarine and sugar and beat in the egg. Add the salt and flour alternately with the milk. Spoon half the dough into a greased baking dish.

Arrange the pie apples on top of the dough. Sprinkle the sultanas and cinnamon sugar over and spoon the rest of the dough on top. Bake for about 30 minutes until golden brown.

Melt the syrup or honey and margarine or butter together and pour, boiling, over the tart as soon as it comes from the oven.

VARIATION

Use 1 can crushed pineapple instead of the pie apples.

Tip

Make baked caramel custard by placing cream caramels (the sweets) in the custard dish, pouring the custard mixture over and baking in the usual way. As the custard cooks, the sweets melt and make a delicious sauce.

Tip

Stew apples for apple tart in orange juice instead of water.

LEFT: Baked chocolate pudding

MOIRA'S PUDDING

750 ml cornflakes

250 ml sugar

125 g margarine, melted

CUSTARD MIXTURE

3 eggs, separated

37,5 ml custard powder

1,25 litres milk

125 ml sugar

30 ml castor sugar

Preheat the oven to 160°C (325°F).

Crush the cornflakes lightly and mix with the sugar and margarine. Set aside.

Mix the egg yolks with the custard powder and 125 ml of the milk.

Boil the rest of the milk. Remove from the stove and stir in the egg yolk mixture. Return to the stove and cook over low heat until thick and cooked. Stir often. Add the ordinary sugar and mix well.

Spoon a layer of cornflake mixture into a greased ovenproof dish and cover with a layer of custard mixture. Repeat the layers until all the ingredients have been used. End with a layer of cornflakes.

Whisk the egg whites with the castor sugar until stiff and spread over the cornflakes. Bake for about 25 minutes or until golden brown.

Serve hot.

Tip

For a healthy alternative, serve baked puddings with a generous helping of vanilla flavoured yoghurt instead of custard.

Tip

Date loaf and hot custard makes for a really delicious dessert.

BAKED CHOCOLATE PUDDING

DOUGH

60 ml margarine, melted

175 ml sugar

1 egg, beaten

5 ml vanilla essence

250 ml cake flour

20 ml cocoa

2 ml salt

10 ml baking powder

175 ml milk

SAUCE

300 ml boiling water

250 ml brown sugar

25 ml cocoa

Preheat the oven to 180°C (350°F).

Beat the margarine and sugar together well. Add the egg and essence. Sift the dry ingredients together and add to the mixture alternately with the milk. Spoon into a greased baking dish.

Mix all the sauce ingredients and boil for a few minutes. Pour carefully over the dough mixture. Bake for 30 minutes.

Serve hot with ice cream, custard or cream.

MICROWAVE METHOD

Mix the dough as instructed. Make the sauce: Microwave on 100% power for 2 minutes, mix well and microwave on 100% power for a further 3 minutes. Pour the sauce over the dough and microwave on 70% power for 10-12 minutes. Cover the pudding as soon as you remove it from the oven and allow to set for 3 minutes.

HONEY CAKE

250 ml cake flour

20 ml baking powder

125 ml sugar

pinch of salt

25 ml margarine

125 ml milk

1 egg, beaten

SYRUP

25 ml margarine

37,5 ml honey or golden syrup

10 ml hot water

pinch of salt

Preheat the oven to 180°C (350°F).

Sift the dry ingredients together. Heat the margarine and milk until lukewarm. Add the egg and mix well. Add the dry ingredients. Pour the batter into a greased baking dish and bake immediately for 15-20 minutes or until golden brown.

Boil all the syrup ingredients together and pour the boiling syrup over the hot cake.

Serve with cream or custard, if desired.

SAGO PUDDING

100 ml sago

750 ml milk

45 ml sugar

15 ml golden syrup

pinch of salt

4 eggs, separated (divide the egg whites into two portions)

25 ml margarine

5 ml vanilla essence

apricot jam

Preheat the oven to 180°C (350°F).

Boil the sago, milk, 15 ml of the sugar, golden syrup and salt together until the sago is transparent and cooked. Stir often. Remove from the stove and allow to cool slightly.

Beat the egg yolks and stir quickly into the mixture with the margarine and essence. Whisk half the egg whites until stiff and fold into the mixture. Spoon into a greased ovenproof dish and bake for 20 minutes.

Spoon a few spoonfuls of jam on top when you remove it from the oven.

Whisk the remaining egg whites until stiff and add the remaining 30 ml sugar, a little at a time. Whisk well after each addition. Spoon over the pudding. Bake for 15 minutes or until the egg whites are golden brown. Serve hot.

SAGO DUMPLINGS

750 ml milk

75 ml sago

pinch of salt

60 ml margarine

50 ml sugar

75 ml cornflour

4 eggs, separated

30 ml butter

cinnamon sugar to taste

Boil 700 ml milk, the sago, salt and margarine together until the sago is soft, transparent and thickened. Stir often to ensure that the mixture will not burn or boil over. Remove from the stove.

Mix the sugar, cornflour and egg yolks with the remaining 50 ml milk. Spoon a little of the hot sago mixture into the cornflour mixture and mix well. Add this mixture to the rest of the sago mixture and stir well. Return to the stove and simmer over low heat until done.

Whisk the egg whites until stiff and fold lightly into the mixture with a metal spoon. Remove from the stove.

Melt the butter. Sprinkle a little cinnamon sugar into the base of a serving dish. Spoon tablespoonfuls of the sago mixture into the serving dish, dipping the spoon in the melted butter each time. Sprinkle cinnamon sugar over each layer of dumplings. Pour the remaining butter over the last layer of dumplings.

Serve hot.

OLD-FASHIONED RICE PUDDING

500 ml cooked rice, cooked until soft

700 ml milk

125 ml sugar

2 eggs, separated

5 ml vanilla essence

125 ml seedless raisins

30 ml castor sugar

Preheat the oven to 180°C (350°F).

Heat the rice, milk and sugar to boiling point and cook until the mixture thickens. Beat the egg yolks and vanilla essence together lightly. Add 30-45 ml of the hot rice mixture to the egg yolk mixture, stirring well. The egg mixture should not be heated too quickly. Add the egg mixture to the rice and allow to cook for a minute. Remove from the stove and add the raisins. Spoon into a greased ovenproof dish.

Whisk the egg whites until stiff. Whisk the castor sugar in gradually until the egg white mixture forms stiff peaks. Cover the rice mixture with the egg white mixture. Bake for about 20 minutes or until the egg white browns.

ORANGE SYRUP CAKE

3 eggs

250 ml sugar

375 ml cake flour

8 ml baking powder

1 ml salt

200 ml milk

37,5 ml cooking oil

SYRUP

375 ml sugar

250 ml water

250 ml fresh orange juice

37,5 ml grated orange peel

Preheat the oven to 180°C (350°F).

Beat the eggs and sugar together well. Sift the flour, baking powder and salt together and add. Heat the milk and oil until fairly warm and add to the egg mixture. Mix well and spoon into a greased baking dish. Bake for 20-25 minutes.

Boil all the syrup ingredients together and pour the boiling syrup over the cake as soon as it comes from the oven. Serve with ice cream.

CHOCOLATE PEACHES

1 large can (820 g) peach halves

Choc Crust biscuits

1 small can cream

Arrange the peaches in an ovenproof dish, hollows facing upwards. Place a Choc Crust biscuit in each hollow and spoon some of the peach syrup over. Allow to stand for about 20 minutes, basting the biscuits once with syrup.

Preheat the oven to 180°C (350°F). Bake the peaches for 12 minutes. Serve hot with lightly whipped canned cream.

BANANA PUDDING

4 eggs

875 ml hot milk

325 ml sugar

250 ml breadcrumbs

5 ml vanilla essence

pinch of salt

5 ripe bananas

12,5 ml apricot jam

Preheat the oven to 180°C (350°F).

Separate two of the eggs. Mix the egg yolks and the other two whole eggs with the hot milk, 250 ml sugar, breadcrumbs, essence, salt and three mashed bananas. Spoon into a greased baking dish and bake for about 20 minutes or until set.

Allow the oven to cool to 150°C (300°F). Spread the jam over the banana mixture. Slice the two remaining bananas and arrange on top of the jam. Whisk the egg whites until stiff and add the remaining 75 ml sugar a little at a time. Whisk well after each addition. Spoon over the banana slices and bake until the egg white is light brown.

QUICK BANANA PUDDING

6 bananas, cut into small pieces

500 ml water

250 ml sugar

30 ml lemon juice

12,5 ml custard powder

500 ml cooked custard

biscuit crumbs or glacé cherries for decoration

Place the first four ingredients in a saucepan and heat to boiling point. Mix the custard powder with a little water and stir in. Stir well and cook until the bananas are soft. Spoon into a dish and pour the cooked custard over. Decorate with biscuit crumbs or cherries. Serve hot.

QUICK PUDDING

SYRUP

250 ml sugar

1 litre boiling water

15 ml sherry

DOUGH

250 g margarine

250 ml sugar

2 eggs

30 ml apricot jam

10 ml ground ginger

15 ml bicarbonate of soda

250 ml lukewarm milk

750 ml cake flour

Dissolve the sugar in the boiling water. Add the sherry and pour the syrup into a deep ovenproof dish with a lid.

Preheat the oven to 220°C (425°F).

Melt the margarine in a saucepan and add the sugar. Stir over low heat until the sugar has dissolved. Remove from the stove. Beat in the eggs and stir in the jam and ginger. Mix the bicarbonate of soda with the milk and stir into the sugar mixture, alternately with the flour, to form a dough.

Spoon the dough into the syrup and cover with the lid. Bake for 1 hour. Serve hot with ice cream or custard.

STELLA 'S MALVA PUDDING

125 ml sugar

15 ml butter or margarine

15 ml apricot jam

1 egg

5 ml bicarbonate of soda

250 ml milk

250 ml cake flour

5 ml vanilla essence

2 ml salt

SAUCE

1 can (410 g) evaporated milk

250 ml sugar

125 g butter or margarine

5 ml vanilla essence

Preheat the oven to 180°C (350°F).

Beat the sugar and butter or margarine until creamy. Add the jam and egg and mix well. Mix the bicarbonate of soda and milk and add to the sugar mixture. Add the flour, essence and salt and mix well. Spoon into a greased ovenproof dish and bake for 30 minutes.

Heat the milk, sugar and butter or margarine in a saucepan and boil together for 5 minutes. Stir well. Remove from the stove and stir in the essence.

Pour the boiling sauce over the pudding as soon as it comes from the oven. Serve hot with custard or ice cream.

MUM'S MELKTERT

CRUST

60 ml sugar

60 g margarine

1 egg, beaten

I ml salt

180 ml cake flour

8 ml baking powder

60 ml milk

FILLING

1 litre milk

60 g margarine

250 ml sugar

30 ml cornflour

30 ml cake flour

2 ml salt

4 eggs, separated

3 ml vanilla essence

ground cinnamon

Beat the sugar and margarine until creamy and add the egg. Mix well. Sift the dry ingredients together and stir into the sugar mixture alternately with the milk. Divide the dough into two and spoon into two greased pie dishes. Spread the dough out evenly in the pie dishes with a spatula.

Preheat the oven to 180°C (350°F).

Prepare the filling. Boil the milk and margarine over low heat. Meanwhile, mix the sugar, cornflour, flour and salt to a paste with a little water. Add the egg yolks and vanilla essence to the paste and mix well. Add a little of the boiling milk to the flour mixture and stir well. Stir the flour mixture into the milk in the saucepan. Stir constantly until the mixture starts to boil and thicken. Remove from the stove. Whisk the egg whites until stiff and fold in with a metal spoon.

Divide the filling into two and spoon into the pie dishes. Sprinkle a little ground cinnamon over. Bake for about 20 minutes.

Pudding sauces

CHOCOLATE SAUCE

250 ml sugar

125 ml water

50 ml cocoa

pinch of cream of tartar

12,5 ml margarine

pinch of salt

3 ml vanilla essence

Boil the sugar, water, cocoa and cream of tartar together well. Stir well. Remove from the stove and stir in the margarine, salt and essence. Serve the sauce hot with ice cream.

MICROWAVE METHOD

Follow the same method and microwave the sauce on 100% power for 4 minutes. Stir well after 2 minutes, then after every minute.

CARAMEL SAUCE

125 ml sugar

5 ml butter or margarine

250 ml hot milk

5 ml cornflour

pinch of salt

cold milk

3 ml vanilla essence

Heat the sugar and butter or margarine until lightly browned and add the hot milk. Stir well until the sugar has dissolved. Mix the cornflour and salt to a paste with a little cold milk and stir into the milk mixture. Cook for 2 minutes. Remove from the stove and add the essence. Serve hot or cold.

INDEX